# The Land and People of
# IRAN

The history of Iran—formerly called Persia—goes back over 2,500 years, to the founding of an empire which at its height reached from the Mediterranean to India. Its story rings with famous names: Cyrus, Darius, Xerxes, Genghis Khan, Tamerlane. As a modern nation, Iran has a rich cultural and artistic heritage that reflects its colorful past. The discovery of oil has brought problems to Iran, but it has brought benefits as well. Thanks to oil and to other new industries, great economic and technological advances are being made, and solutions to current economic and social problems are being sought and found. This newly revised edition gives an account of Iran's "White Revolution" and of her place in today's Arab world.

# PORTRAITS OF THE NATIONS SERIES

THE LAND AND PEOPLE OF AFGHANISTAN

THE LAND AND PEOPLE OF ALGERIA

THE LAND AND PEOPLE OF ARGENTINA

THE LAND AND PEOPLE OF AUSTRALIA

THE LAND AND PEOPLE OF AUSTRIA

THE LAND AND PEOPLE OF THE BALKANS

THE LAND AND PEOPLE OF BELGIUM

THE LAND AND PEOPLE OF BRAZIL

THE LAND AND PEOPLE OF BURMA

THE LAND AND PEOPLE OF CAMBODIA

THE LAND AND PEOPLE OF CANADA

THE LAND AND PEOPLE OF CENTRAL AMERICA

THE LAND AND PEOPLE OF CEYLON

THE LAND AND PEOPLE OF CHILE

THE LAND AND PEOPLE OF CHINA

THE LAND AND PEOPLE OF COLOMBIA

THE LAND AND PEOPLE OF THE CONGO

THE LAND AND PEOPLE OF CUBA

THE LAND AND PEOPLE OF CZECHOSLOVAKIA

THE LAND AND PEOPLE OF DENMARK

THE LAND AND PEOPLE OF EGYPT

THE LAND AND PEOPLE OF ENGLAND

THE LAND AND PEOPLE OF ETHIOPIA

THE LAND AND PEOPLE OF FINLAND

THE LAND AND PEOPLE OF FRANCE

THE LAND AND PEOPLE OF GERMANY

THE LAND AND PEOPLE OF GHANA

THE LAND AND PEOPLE OF GREECE

THE LAND AND PEOPLE OF THE GUIANAS

THE LAND AND PEOPLE OF HOLLAND

THE LAND AND PEOPLE OF HUNGARY

THE LAND AND PEOPLE OF ICELAND

THE LAND AND PEOPLE OF INDIA

THE LAND AND PEOPLE OF INDONESIA

THE LAND AND PEOPLE OF IRAN ✳

THE LAND AND PEOPLE OF IRAQ

THE LAND AND PEOPLE OF IRELAND

THE LAND AND PEOPLE OF ISRAEL

THE LAND AND PEOPLE OF ITALY

THE LAND AND PEOPLE OF JAPAN

THE LAND AND PEOPLE OF JORDAN

THE LAND AND PEOPLE OF KENYA

THE LAND AND PEOPLE OF KOREA

THE LAND AND PEOPLE OF LEBANON

THE LAND AND PEOPLE OF LIBERIA

THE LAND AND PEOPLE OF LIBYA

THE LAND AND PEOPLE OF MALAYSIA

THE LAND AND PEOPLE OF MEXICO

THE LAND AND PEOPLE OF MOROCCO

THE LAND AND PEOPLE OF NEW ZEALAND

THE LAND AND PEOPLE OF NIGERIA

THE LAND AND PEOPLE OF NORWAY

THE LAND AND PEOPLE OF PAKISTAN

THE LAND AND PEOPLE OF PERU

THE LAND AND PEOPLE OF THE PHILIPPINES

THE LAND AND PEOPLE OF POLAND

THE LAND AND PEOPLE OF PORTUGAL

THE LAND AND PEOPLE OF RHODESIA

THE LAND AND PEOPLE OF ROMANIA

THE LAND AND PEOPLE OF RUSSIA

THE LAND AND PEOPLE OF SCOTLAND

THE LAND AND PEOPLE OF SOUTH AFRICA

THE LAND AND PEOPLE OF SPAIN

THE LAND AND PEOPLE OF SWEDEN

THE LAND AND PEOPLE OF SWITZERLAND

THE LAND AND PEOPLE OF SYRIA

THE LAND AND PEOPLE OF TANZANIA

THE LAND AND PEOPLE OF THAILAND

THE LAND AND PEOPLE OF TUNISIA

THE LAND AND PEOPLE OF TURKEY

THE LAND AND PEOPLE OF URUGUAY

THE LAND AND PEOPLE OF VENEZUELA

THE LAND AND PEOPLE OF THE WEST INDIES

*Also in the same format*

THE ISLANDS OF HAWAII

THE ISLAND OF PUERTO RICO

# The Land and People of
# IRAN

by Helen Hinckley

PORTRAITS OF THE NATIONS SERIES

J. B. LIPPINCOTT COMPANY
Philadelphia          New York

*Map by Donald Pitcher*

The author wishes to thank the Iranian Imperial Embassy for the photographs on pages 13, 17, and 21; Helen Barsumian for the photographs
on pages 53, 146, and 149; Ivan Jones for the photographs on pages 66,
84, 106, 107, 109, 120, 121, 125, and 135; CARE for the photographs
on pages 15,. 104, 108, 111, 150, 153, and 154; the Fine Arts Depart-
ment of Iran for the photographs on pages 50, 58, 59, 65, 70, 72, 73,
94, and 137.

U. S. Library of Congress Cataloging in Publication Data

Jones, Helen Hinckley, birth date
    The land and people of Iran.

    (Portraits of the nations series)
    SUMMARY: An introduction to the history, people, customs,
geography, industries, religion, and modern progress of a country
whose history goes back more than 2500 years.


    1. Iran—Juvenile literature. [1. Iran] I. Title.
DS254.5.J6   1973                    915.5                    70-37733
ISBN-0-397-31202-4

# Contents

ONE       The Land       11

TWO       History Is Everywhere       18

THREE       Religion Comes to Iran       28

FOUR       Then Came Alexander the Great       34

FIVE       Water for a Thirsty Land       40

SIX       Islam, Iran's Greatest Invader       51

SEVEN       The Golden Age       61

EIGHT       Shah Abbas and His City of Isfahan       68

NINE       Foreign Infiltration and the Rise       76
of Reza Shah

TEN       Here Are the People       83

ELEVEN       The Nomads       95

TWELVE       The People and the Soil       105

THIRTEEN       Iran's Cities       119

FOURTEEN       Oil and Industry       129

FIFTEEN       Tomorrow in Iran       139

Index       155

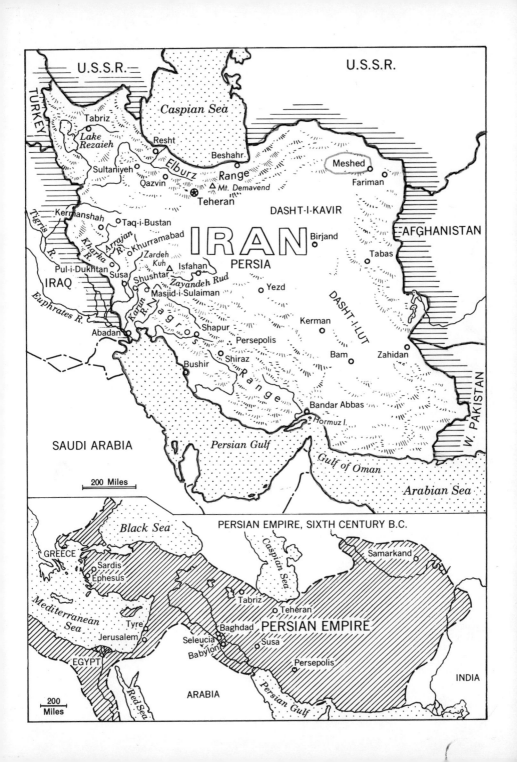

**U.S.S.R.**

**U.S.S.R.**

TURKEY

*Caspian Sea*

Tabriz

*Lake Rezaieh*

Resht

Beshahr

Meshed

Sultaniyeh

*Elburz Range*

Fariman

Qazvin

△ Mt. Demavend

⊛ Teheran

DASHT-I-KAVIR

**AFGHANISTAN**

Kermanshah

Taq-i-Bustan

**IRAN**

Birjand

Tabas

*Tigris R.*

*Kharka R.*

*Arrajan R.*

Khurramabad

*Zardeh Kuh*

△ Isfahan

**PERSIA**

Pul-i-Dukhtan

Susa

Shushtar

*Zayandeh Rud*

Yezd

Masjid-i-Sulaiman

**IRAQ**

*Euphrates R.*

*Karun R.*

*Zagros Range*

Shapur

Kerman

DASHT-I-LUT

Abadan

Persepolis

Bam

Zahidan

Bushir

Shiraz

**W. PAKISTAN**

Bandar Abbas

**SAUDI ARABIA**

Hormuz I.

*Persian Gulf*

*Gulf of Oman*

200 Miles

*Arabian Sea*

PERSIAN EMPIRE, SIXTH CENTURY B.C.

*Black Sea*

*Caspian Sea*

Samarkand

**GREECE**

Sardis

Ephesus

Tabriz

Teheran

*Mediterranean Sea*

Tyre

Jerusalem

Baghdad

Seleucia

Babylon

Susa

**PERSIAN EMPIRE**

**EGYPT**

**INDIA**

200 Miles

**ARABIA**

*Red Sea*

Persepolis

*Persian Gulf*

*One*

# THE LAND

IRAN has two names—Iran and Persia.

Before history began, an Aryan people moved south and west from the territory south of the Aral Sea to a sun-swept, wind-swept plateau south of the Caspian. These people called the plateau Iran, home of the Aryans.

Later, when the Medes and the Persians combined to sweep into the Mesopotamia Valley to the west, the whole region was given the name of the dominant people—Persia. Ferdousi, the great epic poet, writing in the eleventh century A.D., spoke of Iranzamin, which means land of Iran or country of Iran. When Europeans began to get acquainted with the country in modern times they called it Persia, just as the Greeks had when Persia was threatening the lives of the Greek city-states. But in 1935 the government adopted Iran as the official name and asked all foreign nations to use it.

Two names for the same country can be confusing. We speak of the Persian language, Persian art, Persian poetry, Persian architecture, Persian carpets, Persian customs and traditions, Persian people. But when we speak of the great oil industry or of the modern state, we speak of Iran.

In ancient days Iran was a bridge between far Eastern Asia and the land of the Mediterranean and of Europe. The people of Iran were among the earliest in the world to move on to lower land, to form villages, to cultivate crops, to domesticate animals. Their villages lay in the way of wave after wave of migrations. Quietly the Iranians absorbed the newcomers, learning from them, but never giving way before them.

Trade routes crossed northern Iran. Caravans of loaded camels plodded from East to West, from West to East. Later, when sea routes became important, excellent highways led from the coastal ports to the great trading cities that were inland. But in the nineteenth century when the Suez Canal was completed, Iran no longer had a vital role in trade. This phase of her history was ended.

Once, Iran was the greatest empire in the world. Now it is a rather small nation.

Iran covers 636,293 square miles. This is approximately the size of the southwest section of the United States including Texas, New Mexico, Arizona, and California. There are some 20,000,000 people in Iran, which is roughly the same as the population of America's Southwest.

For twelve hundred miles, Russia's frontier stretches along the northern edge of Iran, broken only by the contested waters of the Caspian Sea. To Iran's east are Afghanistan and Pakistan. At the west are Turkey and Iraq, and across the Persian Gulf to the southwest is Saudi Arabia.

The development of Iran has been controlled by its mountains. Two great mountain ranges seem to form a stupendous "wishbone." One side of the wishbone, the Zagros range, incredibly precipitous and craggy, runs north and south the length of Iran near the western frontier. The other, the Elburz, runs almost east and west across the north. The two ranges join above the extreme northwest corner of Iran.

From the air, ridge after ridge of mountains separated by long lateral valleys look like the corrugated surface of an old-fashioned copper washboard. Seen at close range the mountains are vivid in color, and the folding and faulting of the strata is spectacular.

Since the mountains run in regular files, almost paralleling each other for miles upon miles, the valleys between them may be twenty-five to fifty miles long but are seldom more than eight or ten miles wide. The valley bottoms are flat, rising to

Shahnaz Dam which supplies drinking water for Hamadan.

higher ridges before the mountains lift sheer precipices like giant-built fortifications.

The villages are not in the flat-bottomed valleys, but on the higher rims. The roads run down the center of the valleys. Thus village life remains untouched by the world, generation after generation.

The Caspian Sea, lying between Iran and the Soviet Union on the north, is the largest land-locked body of water in the world. Every year it is growing slightly smaller, and although this shrinking has been taking place for untold centuries it is still less salty than the sea, and there are many fish. Much of the world's caviar come from the Caspian. There are no large ports on this sea and sudden, violent storms are a danger to small boats.

In the northwest corner of Iran there is another land-locked sea called Lake Rezaieh. It is about the size of Great Salt Lake and equally as salty. No fish can live in it, but well-to-do Persians camp near its shore to use the mud as a cure for rheumatism, arthritis, and many other troubles.

These lakes would probably be great bodies of fresh water if the rivers of Iran could empty into them. Because of the formation of the mountains, the rivers and streams, fed by the melting snow, flow into the vast inland deserts.

The river Zayandeh Rud is about three hundred feet wide as it passes the city of Isfahan in the spring. In the summer it is barely a trickle. Of course farmers have drawn off its water to flood rice paddies and to irrigate their fields and gardens, but the real reason for its varying flow is the climate. There is seldom a long spring in which the winter snows can melt gradually. Instead, the heat of summer descends at once, the ice and snow melt rapidly, the water rushes down in swollen, turbulent streams for a few brief weeks. All of the

Village fishermen near Bushire weave fishing nets.

water that reaches the desert—the wide-rolling river of the spring and the meandering streamlet of the summer—is soaked up by the thirsty desert and seen no more.

Along Iran's eastern frontier there are several marshy lakes where waterfowl seem to be happy, but in all the country there are not more than ten fresh-water lakes. Perhaps that is why the people of Iran love fountains, and pools, and clear running streams.

One-sixth of Iran is desert, much like the American Southwest. There is a great triangular desert with its apex near Teheran and its base eight hundred miles to the east. The northern part of the desert, Dasht-i-lut, is a naked barren plain. The southern part is Dasht-i-kavir, a salt plain. There are oases in this tremendous desert, but most of it is waste-land—salt flats, rippling sand dunes, bitter playa lakes. A single road crosses it from Yezd to Ferdous.

It is difficult to describe the climate of Iran. Persians will tell you that their country has seven climates. In Teheran the weather is much like that in Salt Lake City, Utah, or Denver, Colorado. There is a cold snowy winter, a brief green spring, a long, dry summer, and a short, brilliant autumn. Through-out Iran the rain falls only in the winter. Over most of the plateau which lies between the two great mountain ranges, the rainfall is less than twelve inches—about that of Nevada or southern California.

In the Caspian area forty to sixty inches of rain falls in a year. The humidity varies from seventy-five per cent in the summer to ninety-one per cent in the winter. Here there are dank jungles like those in tropical lands.

Snow falls in the mountains, blanketing the Elburz and Zagros peaks where it packs in and remains until the abrupt heat of the summer. The snow which falls on the plateau melts quickly. The people of Iran watch anxiously for snow. From it the farmer must get his water for irrigation—in fact, all of the water upon which his life depends. The amount of snow affects the grasslands and thus controls the movements of Iran's two million nomad herdsmen.

It can be cold in Iran—very cold, with the road that leads from Teheran to the Caspian blocked with snow. It can be hot. Readings on the gulf coast have been to 130 degrees, but unofficial reports have recorded even higher temperatures.

Dasht-i-lut is said to be the driest place in the world, where even snakes and lizards cannot live. The Caspian forests are among the dampest places in the world. In some places there is almost no wind, but in the southeast corner of the country the wind may blow day after day for weeks, up to a velocity of sixty miles an hour.

The nature of the land—the wide stretches of silent desert, the rugged mountains separating the long valleys, the wide variations in climate—has not only shaped the workaday lives of the Iranians but is reflected in their poetry, their art, their religion, and in the very character of the people.

**Ahe-Ali Ski Resort near Teheran.**

# Two

# HISTORY
# IS EVERYWHERE

In Iran history is everywhere. If you fly low in a plane you may see thousands of earth mounds, some of them a hundred feet high, where once there were ancient villages. If you travel any road you may come upon the ruins of an ancient city, an ancient palace, an ancient caravanserai, or an ancient shrine. Even the road you travel may be part of the *sang-i-farsh* (carpet of stone) built by Shah Abbas the Great in the sixteenth century.

We do not know how many years people have lived on the southern coast of the Caspian Sea, or on the temperate plateau, but excavations in the caves called Belt and Hotu near Beshahr on the Caspian Sea have uncovered skeletons and flint weapons that were left there more than ten thousand years before Christ. Excavators believe that these early people, sometimes called Caspians, were Nordic, of the very same race that peopled Europe in the same period.

About 6,000 B.C. the Caspians learned to plant crops and

to domesticate animals—they discovered agriculture. They left painted pottery and weapons of polished stone. Three thousand years later they came under the domination of the Mesopotamia Valley. These conquerors had already learned to write, had codified their laws, and knew how to build larger structures than the mud huts of the Caspians.

In a high mound called Tappe Yahya, 600 miles west of the Indus and 600 miles east of Mesopotamia, archeologists have found what may be the ruins of the ancient city of Elam. There they unearthed five rooms of a large building and found six tablets with writing that may be more than five thousand years old. From this writing we know that the city was trading with both the west and the east.

About a thousand years later the Aryans in successive waves displaced or absorbed the Caspians. Five hundred years later the Indo-Europeans moved in from the south and west and established the kingdom of Mitanni.

In 900 B.C. came the Iranians. They spoke an Indo-European language much like ours in basic words: Madar-mother, Dokhtar-daughter. These people seem to have absorbed all of the other people except those who fled to the mountains and became the forefathers of some of the nomadic tribes of today.

The Iranians included the Medes (Mada) and the Persians (Parsa) spoken of in the Bible, as well as other tribes.

Strongest of the ancient Iranian tribes was the Medes. At first the Medes were under the domination of the Assyrians. Then the great king Cyaxares overthrew the Assyrians and built a capital city, Ecbatana, where the modern city of Hamadan now stands. These early people left no artifacts, no written history. They occupied all of the southwestern portion of modern Iran north of the Persian Gulf, but we hear about them only from their enemies. In the Assyrian records there are no accounts of the first battles between themselves and the Medes, but there are clear pictures of towns and buildings carved in the stones which were once a part of the palace of Sargon. The eighth campaign of Sargon in 714 B.C. is described in a written record.

The Greek historians Polybius and Herodotus describe the fabulous palaces of Ecbatana, and Herodotus tells us this story:

One night King Astyages, who inherited the Median throne from Cyaxares, had a wonderful dream. He dreamed that out of his daughter, Mandane, grew a great vine that spread to cover all of Asia. He called in the wise men to interpret the dream. They told him that the dream meant that some day the descendants of Mandane would rule the world. Instead of being happy about the dream, Astyages was worried and angry. He thought that every Mede of noble birth was a potential usurper who must not be allowed to marry Mandane. He decided to marry her to a young prince in a weak vassal state, so Mandane was married to Cambyses, prince of the Persians. When Cyrus was born to Mandane and Cambyses, Astyages sent his chancellor, Harpagus, to kill the baby. Harpagus took the child to the highlands and left him in the care of a cowherd, where Cyrus lived like any other mountain boy.

But when he grew up he became king of the Persians and in 553 B.C. he overthrew his grandfather, Astyages. Cyrus was wise, and instead of humbling the Medes he joined them. The Medes and Persians built the first world empire and the strange dream of Astyages came true. Cyrus defeated the Lydian king, Croesus—reputed to be so wealthy that even today people say, "rich as Croesus"—and extended his rule to all of Asia

**Tomb of Cyrus the Great at Pazargad.**

Minor including the Greek colonies on the Mediterranean shores. He then turned back to Ecbatana. In 539 B.C. he moved west again. This time he besieged Babylon, and conquered the city by diverting the Euphrates River.

After Cyrus died in battle in 529 B.C. his son Cambyses conquered Egypt. In 521 B.C. Darius became king and pushed his way into Europe as far as the Danube River, but was finally pushed back into Asia by the Greeks. In 490 B.C. he was defeated at the Battle of Marathon. In 480 B.C. Xerxes captured Athens and burned it—the greatest mistake he could have made. Later he lost his fleet in the Battle of Salamis.

This great Persian family of kings was called the Achaemenians. When the Achaemenid Empire was at its height a royal road, fifteen hundred miles long, connected Susa with the city of Sardis in Asia Minor. Susa, Babylon, and Ecbatana were government centers, but the real heart of the Achaemenid Empire was the spiritual center, Persepolis, built by Darius.

Just thirty-five miles from Shiraz, the ruins of what was once the greatest capital in the history of the world still fill everyone with awe. When Darius began the construction of Persepolis he was not content to build in the rich plains. Since no higher site was available he built a man-made mountain of stone (perhaps with Egyptian architects). The stones were quarried by hand, dragged to the point of construction, and put in place in the time-defying mountains by an inestimable number of slaves.

This platform juts out from the mountain behind it for more than a thousand feet and it fronts the Plains of Marvdasht for fifteen hundred feet. A double flight of steps leads to the top of the platform, which is, perhaps, fifty feet above the level of the plain. There are more than a hundred steps, three or four cut from a single stone, and the steps are so low and the treads so broad that in the days of the Achaemenid kings their knights could ride their horses to the very top.

At the head of the stair was the "Portal of All Lands" built by Xerxes. Here there were four massive stone columns and four doorways flanked by stone bulls with human heads. East of the portico was the *apadana,* the audience hall. The *apadana* was built on a level higher than the portico, and a double stairway of stone led to it. Two groups of bas-relief figures are still seen in minute detail on the masonry behind the stairs. On one side, in three registers, there are lines of attendants and courtiers. The Persians knew nothing, it seems, of perspective, so figures that are supposed to be behind those in the foreground appear above them. The attendants walk

TOP: Massive sculptured double staircase, seen from the north. Persepolis. MIDDLE: The lion fights the bull. Relief from sculptured staircase. BOTTOM: The Persians wear fluted tiaras and long robes; the Medes wear dome-shaped hats and tunics and trousers.

with folded rugs tucked under their arms and one has the royal footstool strapped to his back—just as they must have walked in real life in the days of Darius. Behind the attendants come the grooms, each with a small prancing pony. At the end comes the king's chariot. Below walk the courtiers with big rings in their left ears. The Persians wear fluted tiaras and long robes girdled at the waist. The Medes wear dome-shaped hats and jackets and trousers. Some of the courtiers are stepping forward to offer flowers. Some seem to be gossiping or arguing with each other. On the other side of the staircase walk the emissaries from all the Empire. The Scythians wear pointed hoods, the Arabs long robes, the Syrians horn-shaped turbans. All are bringing tribute to the king. The variety of these gifts gives a picture of the extent of the empire. There are heavy collars and bracelets. There are weapons—bows and lances and daggers. There are animals—rams, a donkey, a giraffe, camels, a lioness with two cubs, and stallions from Scythia, Cappadocia, and Armenia.

Also in bas-relief we see the royal guard of Persian, Median, and Susian soldiers.

To look with a little imagination at these beautifully carved figures is to turn them into living creatures and to move back in time almost twenty-five hundred years.

The portico of the *apadana* had two rows of six columns each. It is the height of these columns, sixty-five feet, some of them still reaching into the bright blue Persian sky, that makes man seem a pygmy. The columns are made in sections. Each section is so perfectly balanced on the one beneath it that no mortar is needed to hold them together.

East of the *apadana* was once the hall of a hundred columns. The plan of this hall was like that of the *apadana* except that there were ten rows of ten columns each. On the

LEFT: Jamb of northern doorway of the Hall of a Hundred Columns. Persepolis. RIGHT: Xerxes still stands, in the shade of the royal umbrella, looking out over the vast ruins of the Achaemenid palace at Persepolis.

stone jambs of the portals King Xerxes is pictured in many activities. On one jamb he is holding audience with the kings from vassal states. On another he is battling with mythical beasts which represent evil.

There were other buildings on the stone platform: the small winter palace of Xerxes, the larger summer palace, the harem quarters which have been excavated and restored, the royal treasury, the palace of Ataxerxes, and the palace of the queen.

Nowhere in the world is there another Persepolis.

Documents of the Achaemenids were cut into rock and

baked in clay in three languages: Old Persian, Elamite, and Babylonian. And not only these documents and the wonders of Persepolis, were left, but the tomb of Cyrus, the remains of the royal pavilion in Pasargadae, and quantities of beautiful jewelry, bracelets, necklaces, earrings. The jewelry is gold and silver set with lapis lazuli and other precious and semiprecious stones. There are gold and silver coins, each with a portrait of a king. There are human heads cast in bronze and animal heads carved from stone; there are statuettes of gold and silver and bowls of gold and silver decorated with rosettes and lotus buds and flowers.

At the same time that Persepolis was at its height the Achaemenids built a magnificent winter palace at Susa. Archeologists from France and Iran have unearthed a part of the palace and have found two tablets, thirteen inches square and a little more than three inches thick. Darius, who lived from 522 to 485 B.C. had ordered the inscription on these tablets of two royal edicts. From them we learn that the empire included what is now part of India, Russia and Saudi Arabia, as well as Iran, Iraq, Pakistan, Afghanistan, Turkey, Lebanon, Syria, Jordan, Israel and Egypt!

Sometimes people studying the history of Athens and Sparta think of the Persians as barbarians. Actually, the Persians were far in advance of the Greeks in public administration. They were the first people of the world to show tolerance of other races and their customs and traditions and religion.

When Cyrus conquered Babylonia he found the Jews living there in captivity. He sent them back to Jerusalem, carrying their sacred vessels with them so that they could worship in their own way. He even took money from his own treasury to help them to rebuild their ruined temple. The Bible stories of Esther and of Daniel show the relationship of those Jews

**Tomb of Daniel, the Prophet, Suza, Iran.**

who remained to the Persian rulers. Even today there is a tomb known as "Daniel's tomb" near the ruins of Susa. It is considered an Imamzadah (shrine) by Persians living in the vicinity. Daniel rose to the postion of prime minister to Darius and Xerxes; the successor of Darius was the Ahasuerus of the Book of Esther.

What made these Achaemenid kings, so recently desert warriors, so wise, so tolerant? Most historians believe that it happened because they had found a religion far in advance of all other religions of the time—far, far in advance of the religion of the Babylonians or the Assyrians or the Greeks.

They were followers of the prophet Zoroaster.

# Three

# RELIGION COMES
# TO IRAN

No ONE KNOWS when Zoroaster (sometimes called Zarathustra) was born. Most Western historians say that he was born probably in Media in the sixth century B.C. But Dhalla, the Eastern historian, says that the date of his birth is probably far earlier. The language in which Zoroaster wrote his hymns was antiquated when the Achaemenids ruled the great Persian Empire. Only the scholars could read it and translate it into the language spoken by Cyrus, Darius, and Xerxes. There is a closeness in grammar and meter and style between the Rig Veda, the most ancient sacred writing of the Hindus, and the ancient hymns of the Zoroastrians which suggests they may have been written at about the same time. Too, Ahura Mazda, the god of Zoroastrian teachings, was called Mazdaka by the Assyrians, and in 715 B.C. the name Mazdaka appears in the inscriptions of Sargon. Even earlier the name, written Assara Mazas, was on an inscription in Assurbanipal.

Some historians believe that there were two Zoroasters— one who was born in very ancient times and another prophet who took the name of the first great seer in order to spread his religion through the world.

No matter which date is correct for the birth of Zoroaster, his religion was much older than the Empire.

We know nothing of Zoroaster's childhood, but from the hymns he wrote we can guess something about his education. He must have learned all he could from his teachers, and he must have visited the central places where the ancient trade routes crossed and listened to the talk of the travelers from lands distant from his own little world. All that he was taught, all that he heard, was tradition, and to him tradition must have seemed dead while he was alive and longing to push forward. Tradition demands that its teachings be taken on authority, but Zoroaster wanted to study, to ask questions, to *think*.

Zoroaster, traveling from village to city and back to village again, saw that there was misery in his world. He saw that there were greed and wickedness, filth and disease. He wondered if the many gods his people worshipped were worthy of that worship. And so he studied and meditated and went alone into the desert to pray. No one knows how great truths are revealed to prophets, but into the mind and heart of Zoroaster came a new concept.

There was one great and supreme God, just *one*. His name was Ahura Mazda, which means the *Lord Wisdom,* or the *Wise Lord*. Ahura Mazda was never a nature god, never a fire god, though his name became associated with fire.

Even older than the ancient religion were the eternal flames. Under the surface of Iran there are huge lakes of oil, and from these gas arises through the fissures in the earth. Some time before the memory of man this gas was ignited, perhaps by lightning, and a flame that needed no visible fuel burned night and day. Ahura Mazda was *like* the Eternal Flame because he was the source of all goodness and light. As light was the symbol of good, darkness was the symbol of evil. In the eternal battle between good and evil man must take an active part. He can not remain neutral, because if he is not for Ahura Mazda he is against him. The soul is immortal and there is a final judgment for everybody.

Zoroaster wrote many hymns, most of them about Ahura Mazda who is perfect, almighty, absolute, beneficent, changeless, and transcendent. But there are archangels that symbolize the attributes of God: Vohu Manah is the good mind; Asha is righteousness, Sraosha is obedience to divine commandments.

How can people fight for good? Zoroaster's answer was a simple one: Think good thoughts (for thinking and reasoning, Zoroaster believed, was the foundation of all behavior); say good words; do good deeds.

Good thoughts, good words, good deeds. This is a simple creed, but one that made the Achaemenid kings different from other kings. It gave them the tolerance and the respect for the traditions and religions of the people incorporated into the Empire that made them unique among empire builders.

In the Archaeological Museum in Teheran, there are silver plates inscribed at the time of Xerxes and a stone tablet with the same inscription:

"Ahurmazda is the great god who created the earth, the heavens, who created mankind, who created peace for all men, who gave sovereignty to Xerxes to rule the multitudes of men, to legislate for the multitudes of men. . . . Xerxes is the great king, the king of kings. . . ."

Even today, more than twenty-five hundred years later, there are followers of Zoroaster, called Parsees. There are about 150,000 Parsees in the world: 60,000 to 70,000 live in Bombay, 15,000 in Iran, and 5,000 in Karachi.

The Parsees live by the same simple, beautiful code: good thoughts, good words, good deeds. Each Parsee who has been accepted into full membership wears the *sudrah,* a sacred shirt worn under the outer clothing. The *sudrah* is made of fine cotton with short sleeves and a pointed neck. At the v of the neck there is a tiny pocket called the *girehban.* The *girehban* holds meritorious deeds. He also wears the *kushti,* a narrow girdle made of seventy-two threads of lamb's wool. Each thread stands for a book in the sacred scriptures, the *Yazishna.* As the Parsee wraps the *kushti* around his waist three times he thinks: good thoughts, good words, good deeds. When he ties the two ends together he thinks that the body and spirit of man are tied together during this mortal life.

Forgiveness for sin is between man and God, and is achieved through repentance, prayer, and the resolve not to continue in the evil way.

Contrasted with this simple spiritual code, there is an elaborate system of ritual. No one knows how or when the ritual was introduced. It may be as ancient as the first revelation of Zoroaster; it may have been added later to meet the needs of new converts accustomed to a ritualistic religion.

Purity is the quality most to be desired. The clothing of the priest is white. The *sudrah* and *kushti* are white. Dead bodies are dressed in the *sudrah* and in a white robe. The fire temples and the towers of silence are white.

People who are not Parsees cannot go into the fire temples, and Parsees do not tell others what is done there since the ritual is sacred to them. We only know that in these temples the sacred fire is kept burning by special priests.

Since everything in the world is either good or evil, the good is contaminated by coming into contact with evil, and must be cleansed and purified. Ritualistic cleansing is done with "golden water," the urine of a sacred all-white bull that lives in the compound of the fire temple.

While a man is alive both his spirit and his body are good, but three days after the spirit has left the body it begins to decay and is unclean. Not only the dead body but the hands of those who touch it are unclean, and must be washed with "golden water." The body, being unclean, cannot be consigned to any of the good elements—earth, fire, or water. The body, clothed in white, is carried by men appointed to this service to the *tower of silence*. Only the dead and these men appointed may go up the steps, through the iron door and into the tower. Here the body is placed naked on a cement slab. The blood and other liquids drain into a central well and are filtered as they pass through sand, lime, and coal.

Near the towers of silence the black vultures roost in the trees and wait for a body to be exposed. It takes the vultures only a few minutes to leave the white bones to dry in the sun. Sometimes, in some places, the body is devoured by dogs. In every funeral ritual the body is twice shown to four-eyed dogs (dogs with white spots on their faces to simulate extra eyes). The clothing worn by the dead body and by the bearers is destroyed by acid; the bearers are cleansed with golden water and with water and dressed in other clothing before they re-enter the city. In olden times the body was tied to stakes and left on a mountain top. Now the tower of silence is always on a hill. In Iran today there are no towers of silence, and the Parsee dead are buried in the earth, but in Karachi and in Bombay the low towers stand white against the sky and the black vultures, waiting, waiting, waiting, give visitors a peculiar feeling of impending doom.

Though these rites may seem strange to us, they seem reasonable and purposeful to the Parsees.

Wherever Parsees live they are among the most progressive and advanced people. They seek after education, they are industrious, and they are entirely trustworthy. Their women have never been restricted as their Moslem neighbors have been.

When Zoroaster first became "enlightened" and learned that there was one supreme god and that this god was opposed to all of the forces of evil, he taught his belief to anyone who would listen, until it became the state religion of the Achaemenid Empire. Now there is no proselyting—no converts are made. To be a Parsee one must have been born a Parsee. Once it was necessary to close the membership in order to keep the religion "undefiled." Perhaps, sometime, forward-looking Parsees will again follow Zoroaster's instructions to teach the philosophy to everybody.

At the time of the Achaemenid Empire this was a revolutionary religion. The Greeks had many gods who were like men in their passions of jealousy and rage and envy. Even the Hebrews of the Old Testament conceived of their god in terms of their own passions. He was jealous, angry, and especially interested in one group of people.

But Ahura Mazda was above all of these passions. He was as bright as light, as everlasting as the eternal fires. And the Achaemenid kings felt that they ruled because Ahura Mazda had endowed them with power—a power not to be used except in the battle against evil.

*"Ahura Mazda is the great God . . . who gives the sovereignty to Xerxes . . . Xerxes, the great king, the king of kings. . . ."*

# Four

# THEN CAME
# ALEXANDER THE GREAT

IN LESS THAN a hundred years—from Cyrus to Darius the Great—Persia had grown from a vassal state to the greatest of world empires. It had developed a system of government under which people of many races could live peaceably, each race according to its own traditions and customs. It had produced an art that was to be the basis for the decorative skills that would make the Persians the creators of the most beautiful designs in the world. It had embraced a religion so noble, so moral, so forward-looking that it was to influence the religious thinking of the world.

The government depended entirely upon a strong king, because the king, assisted by a council of nobles and a court of law, *was* the government. There were twenty provinces, each administered (not governed) by a satrap, an independent general, and a royal secretary. Each of these checked on the other two. Then there were traveling officials, "the eyes and ears of the king," who reported on all three. There was an orderly tax system, uniform coinage, standard weights and measures.

A relay of horsemen—not unlike the American Pony Express —could carry the king's commands sixteen hundred miles in a single week.

But the time came when the Empire did not have a ruler who could hold this conglomeration together. Many of the kings who followed Darius the Great had grown up in the harem. They were weak, conceited, cruel, inept. Bribery took the place of bravery. Hired soldiers took the place of stout Persians in the field of battle. There were some kings who were better than others, even some periods of reform, but a century and a half after the building of Persepolis the buildings still stood in pride and beauty, but the dynasty of which it had once been the symbol was decaying.

After the Greeks had defeated the Persians at Salamis, and Darius the Great had died while trying to outfit another invasion, the Greeks felt secure from the Persians who had harassed them for so long. They started a series of senseless, weakening wars between the Greek city-states.

Both Persia and Greece were ripe for a conqueror.

And that conqueror, Alexander, was growing up in the mountains of Macedonia, north of the Greek peninsula.

Although the exploits of Alexander the Great are known to everybody, there are varying legends about his birth and parentage which are not so well known. Since he was to conquer Persia these legends have special interest for us.

Ferdousi, in his dramatic epic *Shahnama*, wrote that Alexander was really half Persian, the son of a Persian prince who later became Darab Shah, king of Persia. When Darab defeated Philip of Macedonia in battle, the treaty of peace was consolidated with the marriage of Philip's daughter to the Persian prince and commander. Darab took the Macedonian princess back to Persia with him, but she grew homesick or he tired of her. He sent her back to Macedonia to her father. Alexander was born in Macedonia, the grandson of the Macedonian king and the son of a Persian prince.

Another story, not told by Ferdousi, is that Darab, visiting in the court of Philip, fell in love with Olympius, Philip's beautiful wife. Olympius loved Darab too, and Alexander was born "after nine months, nine days and nine hours" and was not related to King Philip at all.

Still another legend that has nothing to do with Persia is that the God Zeus loved Olympius. Once when Alexander was in Egypt he went alone to a desert shrine to worship. Even the hermit priest stayed outside the cave. When Alexander came away from the shrine the priest knelt to him and said, "Hail, Son of Zeus Ammon."

Obviously, not all of these legends can be true. Perhaps none of them are. To support the legends, we know that Philip and Olympius were always quarreling. To demolish them, we have only to know that Philip took a father's pride in Alexander. Even though Philip, himself, was a great warrior with little education, he brought to Macedonia the great Greek philosopher Aristotle to be Alexander's teacher. Alexander might have been a scientist if he had not been thirsty for conquest.

Alexander began his conquests in Greece and in the areas bordering the Mediterranean Sea. In 333 B.C. at Issus, just inland from the northeastern corner of the Syrian coast, he met the Persian forces commanded by Darius III. Darius III had little of the courage of the earlier Achaemenid rulers. He found fleeing easier than fighting. At Arbela Alexander defeated another Persian army ten times as large as his own.

In 330 B.C. Alexander chased Darius home to Ecbatana, de-

**Alexander the Great and the dying Darius from a manuscript of the Jami by Rashid ad Din.**

feating a Persian army three times the size of his invading army. Now Alexander's victories were becoming legendary. No one could defeat him. Why try? Darius and his army fled to the southern slopes of the Elburz mountains. Alexander was just behind him all the way.

Abruptly the chase halted. Alexander's men brought him the body of Darius, who had been assassinated by one of his followers. Instead of being pleased, Alexander sorrowed and sent the body to the royal family for proper funeral rites.

There must have been something in the arid sweep of Iran, in the sharp blue of the sky, in the bracing air, in the "feel" of the countryside, that spoke deeply to Alexander. In Bactria he married the daughter of a Bactrian noble. Her name was Roshanak—in English, Roxana—and she was beautiful, but whether or not she was loved we do not know. Alexander scarcely paused in his conquests. When he came to the tomb of Cyrus the Great he found that it had been violated. In a rage he ordered the contents restored, and sealed it with his own signet.

Moving on, he married again, this time the eldest daughter of Darius III. He encouraged all of his officers and his ten thousand soldiers to take Persian wives and leave children— part Persian and part Greek (for Alexander thought of himself as Greek)—to be the citizens of a new empire he dreamed of establishing. A Persian-Greek Empire, established on a basis of equality which would incorporate under one government all of the peoples of the earth, was Alexander's dream.

It is difficult to understand why Alexander, with this feeling toward Persia, with this dream of a combined empire, possibly with blood of Persian kings in his veins, ordered the burning of Persepolis in 331 B.C. It is said that he had vowed to burn Persepolis in revenge for the burning of Athens and that he wept as he watched the flames. Recent excavations of the royal treasury have revealed what a tremendous conflagration that was!

But this dream of world empire came to nothing. In Babylonia Alexander took a fever and died at the age of thirty-two. He left the lands he had conquered to his three chief generals. The Seleucids, who received Persia, did not share Alexander's dream. It was said that when Alexander died and was prepared for burial, no band of muslin could hold his hand at his side. As soon as it was bound it would free itself and, bent like a cup, would reach out from the litter on which the body was carried. The wise men said, "His soul cannot rest until the hand is filled," so everybody sought to find what the hand wished to hold. Into it went gold, sapphires, rubies. The hand was not satisfied. Finally a poor old man picked up a fistful of sand and put it into the cupped hand. The fingers closed around the sand and the hand was content to be bound. "Only the dust of the grave is ours after death," the legend says. But old men of Iran, telling this legend to their children, will say, "Alexander loved Persia so much that his hand longed for the feel of Persian sand."

The Seleucids cared little for Persia. Perhaps they envied the Ptolemies of Egypt who were so much nearer home. They built their capital, Seleucia, on the lower Tigris in what is now Iraq, but later they moved it to Antioch in Syria. They had neither the skill to hold the Empire together nor the will to acquire that skill.

Students have always been surprised that in the two centuries of Greek rule the Greeks did not change the Persian art. The Persians have always been able to learn from others whether the others were victors or vanquished, but from the Greeks they learned nothing. This might have been because the Persians themselves had lost interest in decoration since both art and architecture had stemmed from their kings. It might have been because the Seleucids were not interested teachers. Or it might have been because Persian art was already tending toward the decorative while Greek art was totally representational.

Persia, entirely out of touch with the Seleucid rulers, was ripe for a new conquest.

Terence O'Donnell says: "Her dynasties might be overthrown, her palaces burned, her cities heaped with skulls; but the native spirit survived to raise new cities and crown new kings and to impress upon her conquerors the stamp of civilization that remained essentially Persian."

# Five

# WATER FOR
# A THIRSTY LAND

AFTER ALEXANDER died the common people of Iran lived their day-by-day lives in the usual way. They plowed their fields, tended them and harvested their meager crops; they watched their flocks; babies were born and old folks died. It made little difference to them that the Empire was governed by ninety chieftains or that what was once the greatest power in the world had decayed and fallen apart.

But to the warlike tribes on the fringes of the Empire each evidence of weakness was an opportunity for revolt. In the middle of the second century B.C. the Parthians, a nomadic tribe from east of the Caspian, began to strike decisive blows against the already disintegrating Seleucid Empire. Arsaces I began the revolt. Arsaces II established an independent kingdom, and Arsaces III held that kingdom against all attempts to reconquer it.

This kingdom was just a small part of the original Achaemenid Empire which Alexander had conquered. When Mithridates became king he regained Bactria (where Alexander had married the beautiful Roxana), Parsa (where the Achaemenid Empire had begun), Babylonia (where Cyrus had freed the Jews from captivity), Susa, and Media.

At the same time as the Parthians were pushing at the Seleucids from the east a new empire, Rome, was pushing from the west. No wonder that the already decentralized Empire crumbled.

When Mithridates II came to power (123-187 A.D.) he was so successful in war that once again the Empire stretched from India to Armenia. Subject kings continued to reign over their own lands as they had in Achaemenid times so Mithridates II, like Xerxes, took the title of King of Kings.

The Parthians spoke a language similar to the Persian of the Achaemenids. They wrote in an ideographic script called Pahlavi. At first they seemed to adopt the culture of the Greeks, but soon, in the first century A.D., they began to discover the richness of their own heritage. Mazdaism, the worship of Ahura Mazda and the religion of good against evil, light against darkness, became the state religion. The Avesta, the sacred book of the Zoroastrians, was written at this time in Pahlavi script.

At the same time a new influence was making itself felt in the Mediterranean world—in Greece, in Rome, in Egypt, in Asia Minor, even in the western portion of the Empire of the Parthians. This influence was Christianity. The Parthians showed the tolerance of the Achaemenid rulers and allowed the people who wished to, to become Christians.

**Arsaces I**

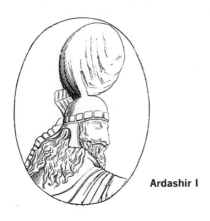

Ardashir I

The Parthian rulers brought artists from all parts of the Empire to the major cities, so there is no true Parthian art. But there was one important architectural development that was to influence Persian architecture—and the architecture of all those who learned from the Persians—until this day. They built the *ivan,* which is a rectangular, tunnel-vaulted hall, open at one end and closed at the other by a wall. This vaulted ceiling was soon to take the place of the flat, pillar-supported roofs of the Achaemenids.

But the Parthian period was to be just a bridge to an even greater dynasty.

The kingdom of Fars had remained independent during the Seleucid period, and when it was brought under the rule of the Parthians the warriors were restless. Were not the rulers of Fars the descendants of the Achaemenid kings? Ardashir of Fars gathered an army against the Parthians. He was not only a descendant of the Achaemenids, but the grandson of the high priest in the temple of Anahita at Istakhr. Ardashir was a successful warrior so he called himself a Sassanian (which means warrior). In 224 A.D. he killed the last of the

Parthian rulers and soon became ruler of all the Empire. Once again Mazdaism became the state religion.

Persia was growing stronger every day, but in the west Rome was growing stronger, too. It was inevitable that the two great powers should fight. Armenia, the center of the struggle, changed hands again and again. Shapur I, son of Ardashir, captured the Roman Emperor Valerian, and held him until his death.

In the cliffs of Naqsh-i-Rustum, near Persepolis, a bold picture of the victorious Shapur and the kneeling Valerian is carved out of the rock. The Persian legends say that Shapur used the back of the only Roman emperor ever to fall into

**The Roman emperor Valerian kneels in surrender to Sassanian king Shapur I (A.D. 260) in a bas relief carved in the rock cliffs of Naqsh-i-Rustum.**

enemy hands as a stepping-block when he mounted his horse.

The Romans had started the war but they could not finish it. The Sassanians could not finish it, either. Rome and Persia shared the known world. Persia stretched from the Mediterranean to India; Rome from the Mediterranean to the British Isles.

Even while these great battles were being fought the warrior kings had time and energy to think of loftier things. Shapur I had the Greek and Latin classics translated into his own language, and Khosrau I gave protection and a royal pension to seven Greek philosophers driven from Byzantium, the eastern capital of the Roman Empire.

The Sassanians did not rebuild Persepolis. Instead they created a new capital at Ctesiphon, near where Baghdad now is.

The audience hall of the palace was one hundred and twenty-one feet high and the vaulted roof spanned eighty-four feet. On the floor, in the winter, was laid the first Persian carpet of history. The carpet was called "The Spring of Khosrau." It was ninety feet square, woven of silk and threads of silver and gold. Woven into the carpet were hundreds of thousands of jewels. Diamonds were used for fountains and streams, emeralds for leaves of plants and of trees, rubies for flowers. There were birds on the carpet, too, their feathers made of precious stones.

Behind a transparent curtain at the end of the hall the king sat on a golden throne supported by legs of emeralds. Above his head the crown was suspended on golden chains, since it was too heavy for any human neck and head.

The crown itself had a history. When Ardashir was crowned, the crown was decorated with pearls. Shapur added other jewels and set a sphere on top to symbolize his addition to the Empire. Shapur II and the kings that followed him each made some addition. The sun was put into the middle of the sphere, and then a crescent moon so that part of the sphere was covered. Bahram IV and Anoushiravan added the star.

Ferdousi writes of the Sassanian kings in the *Shahnameh*, of their love of learning, their religious tolerance. As a young man ascending the throne, Khosrau I said: "We find no fear or lack which sticketh harder at a man than that he should be without a good king." Outside the palace, according to legend, a bell was hung so that anybody with a grievance could ring it to summon the king to hear his complaints. Legend also says that during the reign of Khosrau I the bell was silent for seven years.

Khosrau loved sports. He imported chess from India and polo from the northern grasslands of what is now Russia. These continued to be royal sports. When Bahram was king he imported ten thousand gypsy musicians and scattered them

**Khosrau I receiving tribute from the Romans.**

through the villages and towns so that the common people would have music for their dancing.

It was Anoushiravan who is reputed to have said: "Let it be known to the people that our court is always open to them day and night and we are ready to listen to any petition. Whether asleep or awake, whether hunting or engaged in polo, whether in happiness or illness, the people are always welcome to our court, lest one go to bed broken hearted, for which I shall have to answer to the creator of light."

For although "Magi, Manichaean, Jew, Christian, and all men of whatever religion should be left undisturbed and at peace" (the words of Shapur I quoted from an Armenian source), the real religion was still the worship of Ahura Mazda. After 310 A.D. the priests even named the monarchs, always from the Sassanian line. Two magi lived in each village and there were three great national fires.

But now there was more emphasis on the ritual than on the simple creed of Zoroaster, so new religions began to "break off" from the old. Mani (Manichaeism) was an attempt to make one form of worship from Christianity, Judaism, and Zoroastrianism. Mazdak (Mazdakitism) was an ethical doctrine including worship of Ahura Mazda, nonviolence, vegetarianism, and communal living—a strange mixture of concepts we hear about often today.

In 531 A.D. Khosrau the Just took the power from the priests and restored the hereditary monarchy.

There were in all thirty Sassanian rulers. They built palaces, fire temples, fortresses, dams, bridges, great cities, and the remains of their great buildings can be seen today. Probably the oldest—it may have been built by Ardashir—is the throne room and part of the palace at Firuzabad; the newest, probably built during the fifth century, at Sarvistan sixty miles south of

Shiraz. In addition there are interesting ruins at Shapur, Ctesi-phon, and Qasr-i-Shirin. They brought silk design to such a high point that it may still be seen that the sacred bones of Early Christian saints in many western churches are wrapped in Sassanian silk. They made silver bowls, and jewelry of sur-passing loveliness.

But the greatest gift was water for a dry land.

No one knows when the people of Iran first learned to bring water to their thirsty fields. Only on the rich lowland stretched along the south coast of the Caspian Sea is there enough rain-fall to support agriculture. So perhaps some sort of irrigation is as old as the oldest farming community in Iran.

In countries where there is little rainfall, irrigation water must be drawn from rivers and streams and channeled in canals or ditches to the waiting fields. Or, if the rivers fail,

Varagan IV, engaged in battle.

water must be brought up from underground "water tables."

In Iran the great rivers, swollen when they are fed by melting snow, almost disappear in the summer when the fields are
the thirstiest. To hold the water of the swollen rivers until it
is needed, people from ancient days have built dams and barrages. Ruins of these dams are found in Iran today. Some people believe that they were built in Achaemenid times, but
none have been accurately dated to that period. The dams and
barrages that have been studied appear to have been built by
the Sassanians, who took time off from their wars to improve
the lives of the commonest farmers.

Today great dams are being built to bring more land under
cultivation.

But the method of bringing water from the underground
"water table" in Iran is unique. The Iranians had no pumps,
and the water did not rise freely as in our "flowing wells."
Even if the water had come to the surface readily and had
been channeled in open canals and ditches, the sun would have
drunk it from above and the earth and sand would have sucked
it from below. So the Iranians devised an underground system
of water channels called *qanats*.

As early as the fifth century B.C. (Achaemenid times) the
Persians built such a system in Egypt, so it must have been in
common use in Persia. The system was brought to perfection
in the time of the Sassanians.

Not everyone can build a qanat. The men who build them
in Iran today belong to families that have built them for untold generations.

First an artesian basin must be located. This is a place in
the mountains where an impervious rock layer covers a por-
ous, water-holding layer. A master shaft is sunk through the
impervious layer to the water-holding layer. The water level

in this layer is lower in the summer than in the winter, and the shaft must reach the lower level. This shaft is usually at least two hundred feet deep. One in eastern Iran is nearly a thousand feet deep. It is important that the bottom of the shaft be higher than the land to be irrigated. From the bottom of the shaft horizontal galleries ray out to catch the water from the entire artesian basin.

The workmen complete the shaft and its deep-down galleries and then start work near the village where the water is to be used. On a slight slope the men begin to dig a trench. As the slope rises, the bottom of the trench stays level so the trench soon becomes a tunnel. The usual size is about two and a half feet wide and four feet deep. The trench-tunnel is sighted directly toward the master shaft. About every fifty yards another vertical shaft is opened from the surface of the earth to the tunnel. The dirt that is removed is drawn up by bucket through these vertical shafts, which also furnish air to the men who are working underground.

The dirt is dumped around the hole. From the air one may see these mounds with the hole in the middle like great inverted angelfood pans following a direct line across the desert-like earth.

When the tunnel connects with the master shaft and its galleries the water flows through it, and it is a qanat, not a tunnel. Usually the water will come out above the village in a small stream called a *jube*. This will flow through the village furnishing water for drinking, cooking, washing—every household purpose. After it has supplied the village it will be directed across the fields and gardens.

A qanat may be a few hundred yards long or it may stretch for forty miles. There are two forces that may break down this wonderful system. First, there may be a cave-in; second,

Mazanderan girls taking water from a jube.

the qanat may become clogged with silt. Men must work constantly keeping the channels clear. Sometimes if there is a major breakdown, a new tunnel may be built around the closed area, or even a whole system may be reconstructed if the original system has been allowed to fall into disrepair.

One qanat may water two hundred acres. The Sassanians seem to have succeeded in watering a greater part of their country than is now under irrigation. So in addition to their military successes, their interest in culture and beauty, their prowess at government, they brought water to a thirsty land.

*Six*

# ISLAM, IRAN'S
# GREATEST INVADER

A THOUSAND YEARS had passed since the Achaemenid kings had become rulers of Persia. During this time the Persians had fought with each other and they had battled the Greeks and had been, at first, victorious, but later completely defeated. They had faced the Romans and with the Roman Empire had shared the known world.

One neighbor that had never given them any trouble was Arabia. The Arabs had been simple, nomadic people with no ambition for world power.

But one thousand and twenty years from the time that Cyrus had conquered the Medes and become ruler of the Medes and the Persians, a boy was born in Arabia who would change the whole course of history.

At first no one knew that Mohammed was more than another Arab boy who would grow up to be another camel driver. But Mohammed was an unusual boy who learned from everyone he met. As he accompanied the camel caravans across the wide quiet deserts, he had time to think. As he sat with drivers from other parts of the world, he had time to listen. He liked especially to listen to the religious discussions of the Zoroastrians, the Jews, and the Christians. In the area where he had grown up the people still believed in many gods, both good and evil. The Zoroastrians, the Jews, and the Christians spoke of *one* God. This idea appealed to Mohammed.

As he plodded along beside the caravan or slept under the star-pierced black sky of night, he thought about God. And when he had grown to middle age—according to the belief of his followers—God spoke to him and revealed the Koran. Parts of the Koran were later written by his followers on anything that was handy—even on bits of bark.

At first he told his wife about the wonderful manifestations, then he began to tell others. Some believed, but others were angry. Angriest of all were the priests who made their living from serving the local gods. In 622 A.D. Mohammed was forced to flee from Mecca, his home city, to Medina, in order to save his life and the lives of his followers. This became Year One in the Moslem calendar.

There is a great deal of wisdom in the Koran—much that sounds familiar to the Christian.

A Moslem must *believe* that:

1. There is no God except the All-powerful, the Eternal, the Creator. (Their name for Him is Allah.)
2. Mohammed is the Prophet of God.
3. Justice is the highest human ideal, the most sacred principle.
4. There is a Day of Resurrection and Reckoning on which the good will be rewarded and the evil punished.

Every action in Islam (the correct name for the religion of the Moslems) is VAJEB (actions which must be performed) or MOSTAHAB (actions that should be performed, but it is not

There are many positions for prayer in the oldest mosque in Isfahan.

sinful to neglect them) or MAKRUH (actions that are better not done, but doing them is not a sin) or HARAM (actions that are absolutely forbidden).

A Moslem must *perform* (Vajeb):

1. Prayers five times a day as prescribed by religious laws.
2. Keep the fast during the month of Ramazan.
3. Go on a pilgrimage to Mecca at least once in his lifetime provided he has the financial means, his health is good enough, and the roads are safe.
4. Give alms and charities as prescribed by religious laws.
5. Persuade people to do good and dissuade them from doing evil.
6. Love his parents and relatives, help orphans and lost travelers, visit and comfort the sick.
7. Actively engage in holy wars for the defense of the Islamic faith, his homeland, and his people.

It is this last obligation that changed the Arabs from peaceful tribesmen to some of the most valiant and aggressive warriors in history. It is this last obligation that brought Iran its greatest invader.

When Mohammed died there was a great argument about who should take his place as head of a religion and a people. Some believed the Prophet had said his son-in-law, Ali, should be his successor. Others believed that the oldest of the Prophet's followers, Aboubakr, who was the most respected man among the Goreish tribe, should succeed him. To prevent further trouble, the leaders themselves agreed upon a compromise. Aboubakr was appointed as the first leader, Omar as the second, Osman as the third, and Ali as the fourth.

It was during the time of Omar that the Arabs invaded Iran. In 636 A.D. a Sassanian army of 120,000 men was defeated in a four-day battle of Qadisiyya. Ctesiphon fell and the Arabs spread out all over Iran. But the Sassanians would not give up. Not yet. Another army faced the invaders and was defeated at Nihavand. Finally, in 652, Iranian forces were defeated on the distant Oxus River, and the Arabs held all of Iran. Bands of Arabs moved to Khorasan and settled there. In every household in the captured cities and towns Arab soldiers taught the religion of Mohammed to the conquered peoples.

Of course the invaders would not have moved in so rapidly if some of the people had not welcomed them. Some people felt oppressed by their government. When the Moslems promised social equality and kinder treatment, some of the people accepted them as benefactors rather than conquerors.

But there were others who hated the Arabs in spite of their fine promises. All of the Zoroastrians who could manage to do so moved from Iran into India, where they set up their fire temple and temple of silence in Bombay. Today this is the center of the Parsee (Zoroastrian) religion. Because Omar had ordered the invasion of Iran the Iranians hated him. That was the reason why they were eager for Ali to become the head of Islam. Some say that Ali's son Hussein had married the daughter of the last Sassanian king, so Ali was kindly disposed toward Iran.

In 656, when the ruling caliph was assassinated, Ali became caliph. But he was not to have a peaceful reign. In 661 he was assassinated. His son, Hassan, took his place and he was assassinated. A younger brother of Hassan, Hussein, pressed his claims to the caliphate and he was assassinated. The Shi'ite Moslems believe that the true successor to the spiritual leadership of Islam continued through twelve Imams. Each Imam was considered infallible, each would work miracles, each named his own successor and each died a martyr's death— except the twelfth. While still a young man, the twelfth Imam disappeared into a cave. Shi'ites believe that he will come forth on the day the world ends.

While Ali and his descendants were struggling for the caliphate the actual power in Islam was held first by the Amayyads and then by the Abbassids, who were descendants of Mohammed's uncle.

There are few differences of doctrine between the Shi'ite and Sunni Moslems. The Shi'ites bless the names of Ali, Hassan and Hussein. Shi'a religious men feel that they are inspired by the hidden Imam. But both sects pray in Arabic and follow the words of the Koran.

All through Iran today there are shrines of local saints, called Imamzadehs—sons of the Imams, where people may stop to pray.

During the time that Ali and his successors, the Imams, were struggling for supremacy, the actual spiritual rule was from the Amayyad capital of Damascus, then from the Abbassid capital of Baghdad.

The Abbassids adopted the manners and the dress of the Persians. Baghdad was almost a Persian capital. Once more the invaded had captured the invader. It is not important to trace the political dynasties in Iran at this time. Few lasted as long as a hundred years. But it is important to know what the people were doing.

The Taharids ruled from 820 to 873. They were authors and poets. The secretary of the first Saffarid ruler wrote the first poetry in the Persian language. And during the rule of the Samanid dynasty Abu Ali ibn Sina, known to us as Avicenna, was the first Persian to become a world-famous scientist and philosopher. Two poets, Rudaki and Daqiqi, wrote poetry that seems almost modern today.

Mahmud, who was the seventh of line of Ghaznavids, made his capital in Ghazni. He invited men of learning from all of Iran to come to his court. The greatest man to accept this invitation was Ferdousi. Ferdousi wrote the *Shahnameh,* which we call *Chronicles of the Kings.* He wrote in sixty thousand rhyming couplets the story of four ancient dynasties. Two of these are mythical, drawn largely from the sacred book, the Avesta; but two are historical, drawn from the history of the Parthian and Sassanian rulers. All four are more legend than history, but they are beautiful stories. Ferdousi wrote in Persian, the language of the people, and used few of the Arabic words that were becoming part of the vocabulary. These stories are read with ease in Iran today and many old men, especially in the villages, can recite long passages.

Some learned men wrote in Arabic and some, like Sa'di and Ghazali, wrote in both languages. All used the Arabic script, which was much easier to write and read than Pahlavi.

Mahmud also invited a group of Turks to settle near Bokhara. From the time of the Achaemenids the Turks had tried to push onto the Iranian plateau. Once given a foothold, Tughril Beg, the leader of the Turks, defeated Mahmud and fought his way clear across Iran to Baghdad. The reigning caliph, instead of trying to stand against the Turks, opened the gates of the city and made Tughril Beg "King of East and West." Tughril went back to the Iranian plateau and made his capital at Rey, now just outside of Teheran.

Tughril Beg chose cultured Persians to fill the government posts. He accepted Islam. He became a sponsor of Persian art and culture. One could almost forget that he was a foreigner.

Alp Arslan, Beg's successor and nephew, conquered to the west but was killed by a captive. He left us these unforgettable words:

"Yesterday when I stood on a hill and earth shook beneath me from the greatness of my army and the host of soldiers, I said to myself, 'I am king of the world and none can prevail against me'; wherefore God Almighty hath brought me low by one of the weakest creatures. I ask pardon of Him and repent of this, my thought."

Alp Arslan's son, Malek Shah, established an observatory where Omar Khayyam and other scientists and mathematicians could observe the sky and make a new calendar. He also built a series of schools to advance education.

But Tughril Beg and his successors (the Seljuqs) were Sunni Moslems and they felt it was their duty to destroy the Shi'ites. The Shi'ites, under Hasan as-Sabbah, fled to the mountains. From their fortress there, they made raids on the Seljuqs. From the name of their leader they took the name of "Assassins."

Some say that the "Assassins" were supplied with hashish,

**Minarets and entrance, forming one wall of an Iranian mosque.**

a powerful drug, to give them the courage and strength to stand against the Seljuqs. This is probably legend, since the force of their own convictions plus the dynamic power of their leader would have made them strong enough. They succeeded in killing Nizam al-Mulk and the civil war that followed broke the dynasty's power.

The Seljuq period, although the rulers themselves were not Persians, had been a period of rapid development for Iran. The vazirs, or actual rulers, had been Persians, and many of them had had unusual ability. They had encouraged such philosophers as Al-Ghazali, who introduced into Islam the concept of love as well as justice. They had made it possible for mystic poets like Farid ad-din Attar, and Nizami, who wrote romantic epic poems, to live in ease. People of the West, because of the English translator Fitzgerald, think of Omar Khayyam as being Persia's greatest poet. In fact he was more a scientist, mathematician, and astronomer than poet. His verses are not typical of the Persian nature, but skeptical and even pessimistic.

The Seljuqs, once they had accepted Islam, spent time and money building great mosques. Persian architects planned open courts surrounded by arcades with an *ivan* on each side of the court and a great dome crowning a square chamber. The largest mosque is the Congregational Mosque at Isfahan.

**Mosque at Isfahan.**

It has two dome chambers. At this time, too, tombs took the shape of domes. Many of these tomb towers still survive. Tughril Beg's tomb at Rey still stands.

There were other works of art, too. Many pieces of glazed tile and pottery shows scenes from the *Shahnama* which was familiar to every artisan. The textile workers made beautiful silk, cotton, and woolen materials, and metal smiths worked with love and skill on silver and copper.

Yet in spite of their richness of culture, Iran was broken and torn by civil strife, filled with unrest because of petty injustice, once again ripe and ready to be picked by the hand of a powerful invader.

It had not long to wait.

# Seven

# THE GOLDEN AGE

GENGHIS KHAN, born in 1160, was destined to be the next invader. In 1219 his troops rode into Iran, and never before had there been such a savage massacre. Millions of Iranians died by the sword, were trampled by horses, or roasted in their burning villages. Even the rock-protected mountain fortress of the Assassins was destroyed. There was no one left to fight the victorious Mongols.

Leaving blood-soaked Iran, the Mongols pushed westward into Egypt. Here they were defeated and were forced to retire to Iran to make a permanent settlement.

What happens to barbarians when they conquer a civilized country? Civilization conquers them. The Mongol invaders put by their swords; they even seemed to change their natures. Perhaps it was a settled life that changed them. Perhaps it was the indomitable spirit of Iran, itself, that had known so many invaders and had changed them all to men who loved and honored the Persian culture.

Hulagu, the successor to Genghis Khan, took the title of

Khan of the Tribes, but he named Persians to the high administrative positions and made a place at his court for men of science, for poets, and for artists.

Very soon the Mongols were converted to Islam. By the time that Ghazan Khan, a great grandson of Genghis Khan, became Shah, the Mongols had adopted all that was best in both the Persian and Islamic culture. Iran's Golden Age is said to have begun with Ghazan Khan.

Even now the city of Tabriz, the capital city of Ghazan, reminds us of this Golden Age.

This was the century of growing naval power in Europe. Genoa and Venice, two of the greatest sea powers, had commercial envoys and colonies of merchants in Tabriz. The East was linked with the West by these strengthening water-ways.

When Ghazan Khan died, his tomb was part of a great architectural complex that included a monastery, a hospital, religious schools, an observatory, a library, a palace, an administration building, and an academy of philosophy.

Rashid ad-din was the greatest man of the Golden Age. He was a native Persian who was grand vazir or prime minister for the Shah, physician, and historian. He wrote an important book, completed in 1310, a universal history. Part of Tabriz was called Quarter of Rashid, and thirty thousand houses were built there for theologians, students, artisans, lawyers, and historians.

Several notable poets lived during this period; the greatest of these was Sa'di. Today, in the city of Shiraz, people visit his garden tomb, and many repeat his poems.

Sa'di fought in the Crusades on the side of the Moslems. He was taken prisoner, but luckily he was ransomed and returned to Shiraz. This seemed to have been the end of his career as a soldier, and he settled in Shiraz and wrote great, quiet poetry.

One of his books is called *Gulistan* (Rose Garden), another *Bustan* (Orchard). *Gulistan* is partly prose and partly poetry, but *Bustan* is all poetry. Sa'di wrote of justice, equality, modesty, simplicity, education, prayer, contemplation, moderation —all Christian as well as Moslem ideals. He believed that one should be content with his place in this life and live as virtuously as one can within one's own limitations. He believed in an eternal life in which we shall all be rewarded.

Rumi was a mystic poet who founded the order of the whirling dervishes. The *Mathnavi,* written in rhymed couplets (the same form that Ferdousi used for *Shanama*), is the basic book of the Persian mystics today.

Nasir ad-din of Tus was an astrologer. His instruments were the astrolabe (an instrument for observing the position of the stars and planets), armillary spheres (an instrument made up

**Persian poets.**

of rings representing the important circles of the celestial sphere), and a terrestrial globe which showed the earth to be round. All of these instruments he used at his observatory at Maragha, many years before Columbus! Nasir ad-din wrote on logic, science, and metaphysics as well as commentaries on Euclid, Plato, and Aristotle.

During this Golden Age a new art developed. Islam does not approve of making statues of people, or even using men and women as models for painting. In fact this type of art is strictly *Haram* (forbidden). So artists turned to illuminating texts. This is the art of decorating pages of hand-lettered books. These illuminated texts, generally of the Koran, but also of the works of the poets, are seen in museums today. The pages, often decorated in gold, are inexpressibly beautiful.

Travelers in India are always impressed by the beauty of the buildings of the Mongol period. No wonder. The architects were Persian. Even the most famous tomb of the world, the delicate, phantasy-like Taj Mahal, was designed by Persian architects, though it was built by thousands of Hindu slaves.

In 1380 came another conqueror, Tamerlane the Turk. He conquered Khorasan, Mazanderan, and Sistan and in 1384 Azerbaijan, Georgia (now in Russia), and western Iran, and in 1392, Fars. He moved on into Baghdad and Syria and later into Russian Turkestan and parts of India. When he stopped to found a capital at Samarkand he created a Turkish capital with Persian culture. Tamerlane became a Moslem and became passionately interested in building mosques.

Tamerlane had a wonderful daughter-in-law, the first woman known to have taken an important place in the Iranian culture. Gawhar Shad was so interested in architecture that she worked with Qavam ad-din of Shiraz, and much of the amazing architectural work of the period is due to her interest.

Tomb of Imam Reza in Meshhad, religious center of Shi'a Islam.

At Meshed, the holy city of Islam in eastern Iran, the tomb of Imam Reza dates from this period.

Gawhar Shad's brother-in-law, Baysunghur, was interested in books just as Gawhar was interested in buildings. He supervised illuminators, bookbinders, and copyists at the city of Herat.

Shiraz, now called the garden city of Iran, was the center of learning. Shams ad-din Muhammad Hafiz grew up there, stimulated by the rebirth of culture all around him. While he was still a boy he memorized *all* of the Koran. Hafiz, on the end

**The tomb of Hafiz.**

of his long name, means *the memorizer,* and it is by this name
that he is always known. He wrote six hundred and ninety-
three poems. Even in English translation the reader can feel
the lyricism of the poetry and follow the beautiful imagery.
Sometimes Hafiz is mystic, sometimes almost realistic. His
tomb, like Sa'di's, is in Shiraz. Strangers, looking at the bril-

liantly tiled arcades of his memorial, find a lump in their throats and tears in their eyes. Persians who have problems like to go to the memorial of Hafiz and, in the quiet of the garden, ask their deepest questions. They then open a collection of Hafiz poems and put a finger on a line at random. Many Persians think that the lines of poetry that they find in this accidental way will guide them in their decisions. It is a tradition that shows how close the writings of Hafiz are to the people. And his memorial, so shining and beautiful with its multi-colored glazed tile showing flowers and birds, is an example of the architecture of his own period.

Jami was another great poet of the period who was also a scholar and a mystic.

During the fifteenth century book illustration continued to be the greatest interest of artists. At Herat and at Shiraz there were schools of art. An artist named Bihzad, born about 1400, was the greatest Persian miniature painter. His paintings of people are exquisite in detail and the colors are brilliant and pure. But the faces are entirely without expression. What is even stranger, they are not the faces of Persians, but of Mongols. These faces, popularized during the Mongol period, still dominate contemporary painting. Real Persian faces are beautiful and expressive. Some scholars think that these faces, so unlike those of people the artists actually knew, may not be as *Haram* as actual likenesses.

The four-century period ushered in by the barbaric invasions of Genghis Khan, and divided by the almost equally barbarous invasion of Tamerlane, was still the Golden Age of Iran. There is a spirit in Iran stronger than the ambitions of a warrior. There is no word to express this spirit of beauty that captures the captor and penetrates the darkest recesses of the human mind.

# *Eight*

# SHAH ABBAS AND
# HIS CITY OF ISFAHAN

FOR EIGHT hundred years (four times as long as the United States has been a separate nation) Iran had been ruled by invaders and the sons of invaders. True, these foreigners had adopted Persian ways and encouraged Persian arts and architecture, but still the people must have longed for another ruler like the great Achaemenids.

Shah Isma'il, the head of an order of dervishes in Azerbaijan, controlled seven Turkish tribes. By 1500 he had defeated his neighbors and had had himself crowned at Tabriz. During the next ten years he took Iraq, Fars, Kerman, Hamadan, and Khorasan. National spirit was aroused and perhaps these people wanted to be conquered by Isma'il. Shah Isma'il founded the third Persian dynasty, the Safavid.

Shah Isma'il was a descendant of Ali, so he made the Shi'a sect the national religion. This angered the Sunni Moslems to the west and to the east. They wanted an excuse for invading Iran, anyway. As they pushed at the borders, Iranian national spirit and unity grew.

But with the death of Shah Isma'il the strength of the ruler grew less, and when Shah Abbas took the throne in 1587 the Turks had taken Azerbaijan and in the east the Uzbeks had invaded Khorasan and even taken the Shi'a holy city of Meshed. Shah Abbas signed a treaty with the Turks—a humiliating treaty—so he could spend all of his strength in the east. As soon as he had driven out the Uzbeks he broke the treaty with the Turks and took back Azerbaijan, Armenia, and Georgia.

With his conquests almost completed he settled down to make Iran the great country it had been under former native rulers.

He built his capital city of Isfahan.

Isfahan was not a new city. Legend says that about 1000 B.C. an Iranian king, Tahmureth, noted for his courage, strength, and wisdom, killed all of the giants that were destroying his people and built a city of great beauty and wealth. In 700 B.C. Nebuchadnezzar sent a group of captive Jews to the city (their descendants are still there). The city was called Sepehen until the Arab invasions. The Arabs pronounced it Isfahan (Es-fa-han'). In the center of Isfahan is an enormous square which must have been part of the city from its beginning, since it is mentioned by Ferdousi in the *Shahnama* written in the eleventh century.

When Shah Abbas chose this place for his capital city he made it "half the world." Many travelers in Iran today say that it is still "half the world" in beauty. The Meidan-i-Shah was once a great polo field. Today the marble goal posts still stand, and visitors can imagine the games of polo played in the time of Shah Abbas with expert horsemen and peerless horses. The Shah watched the games from the upper porch of the palace gateway and descended to give the winner a golden cup.

**Part of the great open square that made Isfahan "half the world."**

The square is surrounded entirely by two-story buildings—
some of the most beautiful in the world.

Two of these buildings are mosques. Most mosques in Iran
are open courts surrounded by arcades sometimes two stories
high. Each arcade is a series of niches, much like three-walled
cells open to the court. Each mullah or seminary student has
one of these niches in which to sit and meditate, pray and
study. Just off the courts are *ivans,* shallow arches, lined entirely with beautiful mosaic. From the outside, and seen from
the distance, the domes that cover the arches and the tall
graceful minarets, or prayer towers, are incredibly beautiful.
The Persians love blue of every shade. The dome of the great

Masjid-i-Shah, Royal Mosque, is of azure blue covered with a
darker blue-and-green arabesque of exquisite glazed tile mosaic. Also facing the square is a smaller mosque, the Mosque
of Sheikh Lotfollah, named for a great mullah, but built especially for the women of the Imperial Household. The interior
of this mosque is delicate mosaic faience. Through sixteen
grilled windows the light streams in, making patterns on the
floor. The effect is dazzling, rich, dream-like; yet the spirit of
the mosque is so reverential that everyone falls silent as he
steps inside, and Christian and Moslem alike feel the spirit of
worship.

The Ali Qapu is the palace gate. In those days the gate was
a six-story administration building. Facing the square was an
open throne room where Shah Abbas gave audience to his
people and to foreign emissaries who came from European
countries. Behind the Ali Qapu is a great garden where once
there were many palaces and pavilions. Most of these have
disappeared, but still visitors can imagine the whole from what
is left. The Chehel Sotun, the forty columns, is a palace that
was built by a successor of Shah Abbas. It is now a museum
and visitors can see the open throne room, once lined with
white marble and mirror-work, the smaller rooms, the enclosed throne room behind the open audience room. Half the
columns are actual, the other half are reflections in a pool.
The Persians still love to landscape with pools and with running water. There are many beautiful bridges, but the bridge
of thirty-three arches, with its three levels and special foot-
ways, is the most famous.

While Shah Abbas was building this great city he was busy
doing other things, too. In those times it was necessary to keep
a strong army, and at first Shah Abbas had to depend upon
tribesmen who were responsible not to him but to their own

**Detail from the Royal Mosque at Isfahan.**

Khans. Any time the Khans wished to refuse support, they could. Shah Abbas cut the tribe "rifles" to half, then called for his friends from all the tribes to volunteer for his army. He made a new tribe of these volunteers and called them the Shah Savans, Friends of the Shah. This tribe, no longer a military unit, is an important tribe in Iran today.

Shah Abbas also built roads, canals, caravansaries, and religious colleges. He brought warlike Kurdish tribes to Khorasan and settled them there to make a block against the dangerous Uzbeks. He brought Armenian artisans from Julfa in Azerbaijan and built them a new city, also called Julfa, just outside of Isfahan. There they did their expert textile work, built a cathedral for their own worship, and formed a strong community. Today the Armenians are an important part of the

Armenian Christian Cathedral at Julfa near Isfahan.

Iranian population; they have never been absorbed and although they are Persians they still are Armenians as the Jews still are Jews.

It was not necessary for the religious to take the long trip to Mecca, Shah Abbas thought. They could go to the Shrine of Imam Reza in Meshed. This was made easier by the new roads and caravansaries. Once Shah Abbas walked eight hundred miles to the shrine of Imam Reza. He, himself, trimmed the thousand candles that lighted the sacred court. Sheikh Bahai wrote:

> The angels from the high heavens gather like moths
> O'er the candles lighted in the Paradise-like tomb.
> Oh, trimmer, manipulate the scissors with care
> Or else thou mayest clip the wings of Gabriel.

There were other shrines, too, like Najaf, which is now in Iraq but was at that time in Persia. When Shah Abbas visited Najaf he, personally, swept the tomb of his ancestor, Ali. In Iran the sweeper bends low and sweeps with a soft hand brush made of rushes, so sweeping is an example of humility.

Legend says that Shah Abbas put on old clothing at night and wandered the streets carrying the begging bowl of the very poor. As a beggar he talked with people on the street about their king. He found out what the people expected of him. It is said that many of his policies were based on the needs of the people that he discovered in this way.

The only portrait that we have of him is painted on the wall of the monumental entrance to the northern end of the square where he is pictured defeating the Uzbeks. He was a handsome man with strong, clean features, keen wary eyes, and huge, frightening black mustaches.

At the same time as Elizabethan Englishmen were venturing westward, Sir Anthony Shirley and his brother Robert, with twenty-six followers, offered their services to Shah Abbas. They subsequently represented Iran in many diplomatic posts. Sir Anthony wrote: "His furniture of mind is infinitely royal, wise, valiant, liberal, temperate, merciful, and an exceeding lover of justice, embracing other virtues as far from pride and vanitie as from all unprincely signs or acts."

In spite of his great achievements, Shah Abbas lived in fear of losing his throne. He had gained it through the trickery of his "protectors" and he was afraid he would lose it through the trickery of others. He had his most ambitious sons killed, and those he allowed to live were not trained for kingship. When he died, the power of the empire died with him.

The poets wrote then of noble submission, rather than of action; and of escape into phantasy rather than the facing up to reality. But textiles had never been more beautiful, the work of other artisans was superb, and the architecture has never been surpassed. By 1694—less than two hundred years from the emergence of Shah Isma'il—the revolt of the tribes began and Iran was ready for another invasion.

*Nine*

# FOREIGN INFILTRATION
# AND THE RISE
# OF REZA SHAH

THE EIGHTEENTH CENTURY in Iran was one of turbulence and rapid changes of dynasty. The nineteenth century was one of exploitation and misery.

Nadir Shah, who came to the throne in 1736, had once been a saddle-maker. He soon became a robber baron, then a royal regent, and finally grabbed the throne for himself. While he was Shah he conducted a successful military expedition into India and brought back the Peacock Throne. People in Iran will show you this throne in the heavily guarded crown jewel museum in the Bank Melli. People in India will tell you that the throne in Iran is not the Peacock Throne at all. They say that the greedy Shah Nadir had the throne destroyed for the jewels that were in it and that the throne now on exhibition in Iran is a substitute made of less valuable jewels. Although he was successful in this expedition, he never did anything for his people.

In 1750 Karim Khan, who was the chief of one of the nomadic tribes—the Zand tribe—seized power and made Shiraz his capital.

In 1779 Agha Muhammad Khan seized power. He was of the Qajar tribe—one of the seven Turkish tribes that had supported Isma'il, the first Safavid ruler. Muhammad was a violent man, incredibly cruel. Once one of his enemies fled to Kerman where he was given shelter. Muhammad punished Kerman by putting out the eyes of twenty thousand of its inhabitants.

His violence made him a successful warrior, and by 1797 he had conquered all of Iran. He died before he could enjoy his conquests and his nephew, Fath'Ali Shah, took the throne. Fath'Ali was not a warrior, not a builder, not an alert ruler. He did nothing for his country or its people. Instead there was growing corruption in his government and he willingly signed his name to pacts which ruined Iran.

During the nineteenth century European governments moved to gain power, markets, and prestige in countries whose culture was much older than theirs, but which had been weakened by some internal cause.

Russia made the first move into Iran, annexing the rich province of Georgia in 1801. In 1813 Iran confirmed the Russian possession of Georgia and Russia grew bolder. In 1826 Russia took three more provinces, and reserved for herself military navigation on the Caspian Sea. The portion of the Iranian fleet which had occupied these waters was withdrawn.

While Russia was making these moves to control Iran, France was busy too. In 1807 France made a treaty with Iran, but France couldn't push her demands because of a change in her government.

In 1834 there was  change of rulers in Iran. Muhammad took the throne from Fath'Ali Shah, but there was no change in the pattern of Iran's humiliation.

England wanted to control the Persian Gulf because she already controlled India. Russia wanted to gain control of large parts of Iran because she wanted to expand into Asia. Nasir ad-din Shah, son of Muhammad Shah, took the throne at the age of sixteen. During his reign Russia grew stronger and stronger in Iran and the British forced Iran to recognize Afghanistan, which had long been a part of Iran, as an independent nation.

But even more dangerous was the quiet penetration into Iran's economic life. A British banker got the concession to build railroads and streetcar lines. Another British agent received the concession to run the Imperial Bank of Persia.

Russia countered by demanding that the Persian Cossacks that guarded Teheran must be officered by Russians. By 1900 fifteen foreign countries had special rights in Iran.

Nasir ad-din Shah did not seem to realize what he was doing to his country. Twice he visited Europe and came back and said that all Iran needed to do was to change everything and follow Western ways. The people did not agree with him, and in 1896 he was assassinated.

His son, Muzaffar ad-din Shah, liked Europe, too. His numerous trips impoverished the country. Public servants received no salaries. The only rich men were the nobles and landlords who exploited the peasants. The idle people lived in luxury. Those who worked hardest were hungriest.

By 1906 the people could stand this sort of thing no longer. Ten thousand of them flocked to the British Embassy for protection. The mullahs left Teheran. The bazaars were closed. Nowhere in the capital was there a place to worship or a place to buy food or clothing.

This demonstration opened the eyes of the Shah. He promised reforms, a constitution was drawn up and a parliament (Majlis) was organized to deal with the serious problems that had overtaken the country.

Over the main entrance to the Parliament Building is written: ADL-EL MOZAFFER. This, translated, means the Justice of Mozaffer. But it means something else, too. In Persian every letter has a corresponding number. When the numerical value of the letters are added together we have 1324, the year by the Moslem calendar that the constitution was granted. 1324 is 1906 in our calendar. But even a new constitution and a Parliament did not solve the problems of Iran. In 1907 Mozaffer ad-din died. The common people of Iran will still tell you that he died by some foul means. The truth is that he was sick and died in bed.

His son took his place. He proclaimed that Parliament was dissolved and the constitution discarded. He even bombarded the Parliament, with help from his Russian mercenaries.

This, the people would not tolerate. A liberal army moved into Teheran and Muhammad Ali Shah hurried to Russia. His eleven-year-old son, Ahmad Shah, was ruler.

Finances were in such a state that an American banker was engaged to straighten them out, but Russia was opposed to an American in this position. The Russians even bombed Meshed, the shrine of Imam Reza.

Never had Iran been so much in need of a strong, intelligent ruler.

Reza Khan was born near the Caspian Sea on March 16, 1878. His father and grandfather had been in the Persian Army, so it was natural for him to plan a career in the army. Reza advanced through the ranks because he had special ability and a strong character. When government by the Qajar Shahs became intolerable, when all of Iran was divided into spheres of influence, troops led by Reza Khan marched into the city of Qazvin.

Reza, because of his ability, was soon made minister of war. Finally in 1923 he became prime minister. Ahmad Shah left Iran for Europe and in 1925 a constitutional assembly chose Reza Khan to be Shah of Iran. In 1926 he was crowned, the first of the Pahlavi dynasty.

Reza felt pride, as every true Persian does, in the glorious past of his country. He felt the lethargy and weakness of the Qajar kings was intolerable. He wanted everybody to feel a stirring of new pride and interest that would make for national unity. First, he knew, he must throw off the influence of foreign nations. Next, he must so manage the economy that the country might prosper. All over the world people were feeling the effects of an international depression, which fell heavily upon Iran. Reza's government established industries, it built roads, it constructed one of the most amazing railroads in the world from the Persian Gulf to the Caspian Sea. But he had started at the wrong end of the economy. Agriculture and irrigation—which should have been the first consideration—were not considered at all. Perhaps, having grown up in the rich Mazandaran area, he took agriculture for granted; perhaps, remembering the warm rains of his homeland, he didn't understand the need for irrigation in the rest of Iran. The people in the villages were not touched by the industries, they did not need the roads, they could not travel by the trains. They grew poorer and poorer.

Large sums of money and title to many farm villages came into Reza's hands. Parliament did exactly as he suggested. Only the nomadic tribes were unwilling to give up their freedom. Reza put down the revolts of the tribes with cruelty, moved many of the Khans to Teheran where he could keep an eye on them. These things he did because he felt they were for the good of the country. Public opinion, free speech, might

**Reza Shah.**

slow his work. He abolished them. Highly trained administrators might take over key positions and oppose him; he ne-
glected the training of such administrators.

Still, single-handed, he was bringing Iran abreast of the
rest of the world. He said that women were people, too, and
that they must put aside the *chador,* a kind of shawl that cov-

ered the face of women when they were outside their homes. He made many other reforms.

And then came World War II. Reza had nothing to do with this war. He was content to build his nation, now officially called Iran; to keep clear of foreign entanglements. But Iran was on a pathway that the allies needed—through Iran England could get supplies to Russia's front. Reza liked Germany: German engineers had built his great railroad, German individuals were important to Iranian trade. He also hated Communism and did not want to do anything to help the Russians. He declared that Iran was neutral.

Then, August 26, 1941, Russian forces marched into Iran from the northwest and English forces marched in from Iraq. The British Navy atacked the Iranian Navy in the Persian Gulf. The engagement was over in three days. Reza abdicated at the request of Great Britain and was taken to South Africa, where he died in exile. Today, standing at his tomb, you can almost feel the spirit of this man who loved Iran so much and did so much for the country he loved.

When Reza was hurried away to exile his son Muhammad Reza, became Shah. We will learn more about him as we follow the developments in today's Iran.

# Ten

# HERE ARE THE PEOPLE

SHAHS MAY COME and Shahs may go. Dynasties may rise and fall, invasions may change the boundaries of the Empire, but still in a country like Iran the people living in the villages and the poor people living in the cities notice little change in their lives. Some seasons are hungrier than others, but "Is not this the way of all life?" they ask philosophically.

The common people work very hard and have very little. In the mountain villages where the winters are cold and long, the men's clothing is so patched that it is impossible to tell which is patch and which is original jacket. The village women wrap themselves in *chadors* from head to foot and one can only guess at the rags that are hidden. Where summer lasts all year the villagers wear few clothes; many boys are dressed only in a short undershirt.

The greatest fault of the people is that they have not learned to cooperate with each other. Each man is afraid to trust the other. Yet they are hospitable. There is always a cup of tea for friend or stranger. Sometimes there are apricot seeds, all shelled, or dried watermelon seeds. There is a special skill in breaking this seed with the teeth and taking out the delicate kernel with the tongue.

The people love their children. Babies, who are never heard to cry, are carried on the backs of their mothers; even a little girl ties her baby brother or sister on her back when she goes out to play. The families love their ancient grandparents, too, and turn to them for advice when there are problems.

Yet much as the people love their children, many cannot give them the food and clothing they need. A mother of several sons has to choose each year which son shall go to the village school, since the family has but one pair of shoes.

**Everywhere in Iran little children are responsible for smaller brothers and sisters. Children in the village of Sarbandan.**

The children play games similar to those of American children, and if life gets too hard for the grownups there are always special events, special holidays.

The biggest event in any girl's life is her wedding. Weddings are not exactly the same in all the villages and cities. The clothing the bride wears, her dowry, the groom's gift to the bride's mother and to the bride—all of these may differ, but the similarities are much greater than the differences. In the cities, except among the most modern folks, the parents arrange the marriage. After all, aren't the parents wiser than the young people? In the villages the boys and girls have worked together in the fields and they may let their parents know whom they want for a mate. In the larger towns the bride and groom may be complete strangers until the wedding is arranged.

Ordinarily the boy's mother will call at the home of the girl. The girl will serve the visitor tea and a decision is made at once. If the mother has liked the girl she may send the boy to call. In some villages this is never done, and the groom gets his first glimpse of the bride in a mirror at the wedding ceremony. Both sets of parents will discuss the marriage and come to agreement on all of the arrangements.

Then the sewing for the bride will begin. If the family is wealthy there will be a fabulous dowry. If she is poor she will have a new dress—often a red one—and a white veil. In Baluchistan the bride makes herself a wonderful coat covered every inch with embroidery. These bridal coats are famous the world around.

The groom's family sends gifts to the bride. If the family is rich there will be a ring with a stupendous diamond, for the Persians love jewels and have the finest in the world in their royal collection in Teheran. The next gift will be a copy of the Koran. Perhaps this will be a priceless book, written by hand with every page decorated with gold. Later there will be other gifts—candlesticks, trays, lacquered chests, a samovar. If the groom's family is poor perhaps the only gift will be a samovar. This is a beautiful metal container—perhaps of silver or copper—a foot or maybe two feet high in which water is always kept boiling for tea.

Friends will send gifts by special messenger. These bearers walk in single file, each carrying on his head a tray of bridal gifts. People, especially strangers, stop to watch these processions.

Sometimes the bride stays in the home of her mother for as long as a year getting ready. Finally the day comes! The bride's friends go with her to the bath house and she spends the day in bathing, in shampooing and arranging her hair, in being massaged. A band made up of drums and stringed instruments plays outside and inside the girls laugh and talk and drink fruit juices and eat fruit and cucumbers.

Two mullahs, Moslem religious men, come to perform the ceremony and draw up the contract.

The veiled bride sits on the floor facing toward Mecca, her eyes on the Koran she holds in her hands. Before her on the floor is a mirror, as beautiful and ornate as the family can afford. In this mirror, in old times, the bride and groom caught their first glimpse of each other. The other things on the carpet before her differ from village to village, from one section to another. Usually there is a dish of water in which a green leaf is floating, yoghurt, a long loaf of Persian bread sometimes decorated with incense. There is always a candelabrum or perhaps two flanking the mirror.

The mullah asks the girl if she will take this boy for her husband. She does not answer—that would make her look too eager—but keeps her eyes on the Koran. Again he asks her. She is still silent. On the third repetition of the question she whispers "Yes," and a little squeal goes up from the women, usually seated in a side room, and a clapping of hands from the men who are seated in the same room with the bridal couple. Now two women come forward. One rubs cubes of sugar between her hands, scattering the sugar. This will "sweeten" the bride. The other sews in the air with a needle and thread. She is sewing up the mouths of people who may criticize the bride.

Then the bride and groom watch their parents accept the marriage contract—nowadays many young people sign their own contracts—and the bride is taken to the home of the groom. Sometimes she rides on a gaily-decorated horse. Sometimes she walks. But always there is a procession. On this day she feels and looks like a queen. Her friends laugh and dance in their bright dresses. It is a time for happiness.

In the big cities many weddings are not in the traditional manner. But in the villages and among the families that honor tradition, they change little from generation to generation.

In many villages there is a celebration when each baby boy is seven days old. The local barber circumcises the baby; everybody dances, sings, and eats. It is a fine day for everybody but the baby.

Perhaps it is not right to call a funeral a celebration, but it is a break in the monotony of life. In Iran mourning aloud is expected. Passing a house where there has been a death one can hear the weeping and crying even though the house may be set in a garden behind a thick wall. The body is washed for burial and prepared in a special way. Usually it is wrapped in a length of cloth. Wealthy women may be wrapped in almost priceless Persian materials. A band of material goes around the head, covering and closing the eyes. The arms are bound to the sides of the body at the wrists, and the ankles are bound together. The men follow the body to the grave. Sometimes it is carried—at other times it is taken by funeral car. Anyone who sees the funeral procession go by must take seven steps in the direction the procession is going. This helps him to remember that he, too, will some day go in this way.

The Koran says that the body must be returned to the dust, so there is no coffin. A three-sided box is placed over the body so that when the grave is filled it will be protected. All this time the mourning and weeping goes on.

After the burial the funeral procession returns to the home. Here there is a mullah to read words of comfort from the Koran. A cloth is spread in even the humblest home and on the cloth there are fruit, bread, yoghurt, sweets. For three days the mourning goes on, generally with men in one place and women in another. On the third day the cloth is folded to show that the mourning is over. After seven days the people come together again to mourn and visit and eat. On the fortieth day there is another time of mourning, and on the first yearly anniversary there is another.

In the village this time of mourning can be a very simple pause in the year's work to honor the one that has gone and to comfort the family. In the city it is often almost a social period. Women always wear black, but their *chadors* may be of exquisite lace and their dresses the latest in Western fashion.

These are Moslem funeral rites. The Armenian Christians, the other Christians, the Jews, and the Zoroastrians all have their own rites; but since ninety per cent of the people are Moslem this is the prevalent custom.

For Moslems there are many religious holidays: the birth of Mohammed, of Ali, of the twelfth Imam; the martyrdom of Hussein, Hassan, and Ali, special events in the life of Mohammed and the Imams. Two of these holidays last a month.

Muharram is the first month of the Hegira lunar calendar. (The Persians really have three calendars: the lunar, the solar, and the Western used by the rest of the world.) Many years ago on the tenth day of this month Hussein, the grandson of Mohammed and the son of Ali, was martyred. During the first ten days of the month the people have a special morbid celebration. The place where this celebration is held is called the Rosekhana, and the black flag that flies over the place is the Alam-E-Seyah. A professional priest storyteller called Rowzeh Khan tells the story of the torture and martyrdom of Hussein, and the people grow more and more excited. Later there may be a play called *Tazzieh* which presents these events with such realism that the people's excitement explodes into action. They form processions and march toward the bazaars. Some of the men beat themselves with chains so that blood runs from their heads and their backs.

When Reza became Shah he said these emotional practices had to stop. Still the people spent the first ten days of Muharram in the same way, but in secret. Now, in almost every village and in places in the cities, these strange, painful celebrations still go on.

Ramazan is the ninth month of the Moslem lunar calendar. During this month the people fast from sunrise to sunset because, centuries ago, Mohammed received most of the Koran at this time and the celebration is in gratitude to God for this gift. Also Mohammed fasted in the wilderness and during this month the people share his hunger. At certain times the Koran is read from every minaret. (Now it is read over a loudspeaker that fills the cities with sonorous sound.) The month of fasting ends with a great feast. Even in the poorest home there is some special food for the occasion, and sometimes

**Mosque at Kum, a pilgrimage holy city.**

beneficent people pass out food as the worshipers leave the mosque at the end of the fast.

But the greatest of all holidays in Iran is *No-Ruz* (the New Day or, as we would say, the New Year). No-Ruz is the first day of the month of Farvardin, the first month in the ancient solar calendar. For us in America, it is the 21st of March or the first day of spring.

Once upon a time—so Ferdousi tells us—there was a great king named Jamshid. He rid the country of wicked giants and after he had done that he built a golden throne and invited his people and emissaries from all of the other countries to come to see him sit on this throne. When he sat on the throne, all dressed in silk studded with jewels, a shaft of sunlight fell on his face making it look like the face of an immortal. Then the people knew that it was right for him to be Shah-an-shah (King of Kings). After this everybody sang and danced and drank and dined.

The kings following Jamshid, taking the title of Shah-an-shah, always celebrated No-Ruz. At Persepolis we can see emissaries from every land bringing No-Ruz gifts to the Achaemenid kings. The Sassanian kings always used this day to give audience to their grand vazirs and emissaries from foreign countries. Even today the Shah receives very important persons in the Gulistan Palace.

When the Moslems first conquered Iran they tried to stop the No-Ruz celebration. Singing and dancing were both *Haram* (ninety-nine times prohibited), but soon the celebration began again and now it is the high point of the year.

Preparations for No-Ruz begin a month ahead with housecleaning, painting, gardening, sewing, shopping, cooking. Fifteen days before No-Ruz the family prepares the *sabzeh*.

(This is a plate of wheat or barley seeds that germinate in water and grow several inches tall by No-Ruz. Sometimes the seeds are grown on the outside of an earthenware pot.) Every family must have one of these.

The Wednesday before No-Ruz each family lights at least three small bonfires in their courtyard. Every member of the family jumps over these little fires repeating an incantation: "My yellowness (sickness) to you. Your redness (health) to me." In some villages, instead of jumping over fire, the people jump over water to leave their weaknesses in the stream.

In some parts of Iran women who have illness in their homes go from door to door beating a spoon upon a brass bowl and collecting the ingredients for a soup to cure the sick. They are heavily veiled so no one knows them. Children, to imitate these women, disguise themselves and go from door to door asking for something in their bowls just as American children go "trick or treating."

But at last it is No-Ruz and the families gather to wait for the booming of the cannon that will announce the vernal equinox at the exact second. The cannon roars and the celebration begins. Everyone, wearing at least one new item of clothing, presents himself to the head of his family and receives a gift— a coin, a bit of jewelry, a toy, even a beautiful plant or cut flower.

In the traditional Persian home there is no table. The cloth is spread upon the floor. Since in most homes there is either a beautiful Persian carpet or a *gleam* (a woven rug), and since no one comes into the house with shoes on, this is a nice way to spread the banquet. There must be at least seven foods beginning with the letter s. Some of these are vinegar, garlic, sumac, apple, jujube fruit, smoked fish, olives, a sweet pudding made of wheat, and, of course, the *sabzeh*. There are, too, a bowl with a goldfish in it, silver (another s since the Persian word for silver is *seem*), a mirror, a jar of rosewater, a lamp, a Koran, a bowl of gaily-colored eggs, yoghurt, and cheese.

During the first few days of No-Ruz relatives visit relatives. Later, friends and neighbors visit friends and neighbors. Often there is gift-giving, especially to the children, and always there must be food enough for everybody. Sometimes each person seated at the cloth has someone kneeling behind him, reaching over his shoulder to fill a plate, with much laughter and happy talking. Motorists drive close to the traffic policemen and give them money. There are extra money and new clothes for household servants. For a short time everyone seems rich.

But the thirteenth day is the best of all. On this day, *Sizdah-Bedar* ('thirteenth day out"), everybody, including the royal family, goes on a picnic. In the cities the rich people get in their cars and ride to the mountains or out into the country. Those not so rich ride the buses to the end of the line. Those with no bus fare simply picnic on the streets and sidewalks. Of course it is easy for the villagers to go out into the fields.

The Persians respect the grass. They know how hard it is for grass to grow. They don't picnic on the grass, they picnic near it, where they can see and enjoy it. Sometimes large families ride camels to the picnic. Seventeen people on three camels is quite a crowd even when the last little boy hangs on to the last camel's tail. With every picnic party goes not only a hamper of food but a samovar, for what is a picnic without tea?

On the streets, mingling with the crowds, are clowns and dancers, balloon sellers and folk singers. No where is there a sad face.

The big event is throwing the *sabzeh* (the grain that has germinated and grown) into a running stream. With the *sab-*

ABOVE AND BELOW: Dancers celebrating the tea harvest.

*zeh* go bad luck, misfortune, old quarrels, old unhappiness.

No, life is not easy in Iran, but there are special times of sorrow, special times of happiness. Life is not too monotonous.

# Eleven

# THE NOMADS

ALWAYS, in Iran, there is green grass growing somewhere; and more than two million people, nomadic tribesmen, depend upon this grass. In winter the grass grows green and tall on the lowlands along the Iranian border and the shores of the Persian Gulf. Here the tribesmen till and plant, cultivate and harvest their wheat, and live in their tents of black goat hair. The tents have vertical sidewalls, slightly sloping roofs supported by poles, and earthen floors covered with rugs of woven wool or felt mats. These tents are as comfortable as the homes of the poor anywhere in Iran. The housewives keep these portable homes as neat as possible. In the daytime the blankets are shaken out in the sun and then folded neatly against one tent wall. The copper utensils, especially the samovar, are kept shining bright. In the tent, also, are goatskin bags holding the day's supply of milk or yoghurt, and tall earthen jugs used for the day's water supply. There may be bags of grain and chests for the family clothing. Always there is a cradle of wood. The tribesmen love their children and the families are large and almost always happy. The children obey the father absolutely. The wife does, too, because these are primitive people not interested in the rights of women. Brothers stick to brothers and protect their sisters because of affection as well as from a sense of duty.

In the tents there is singing and reciting of ballads and telling of long, continued stories. The boys learn to shoot because men are counted as "rifles" in the tribes, just as families are counted as "tents."

This seems an ideal life. But in the early spring a shiver runs up and down the spine of the Zagros mountain range. On the other side of this rocky, precipitous arm of the mountain wishbone, the snows are beginning to melt and grass is piercing the winter blanket. Soon the grass on the lowlands will be baked brown under a summer sun. The tribes must move to the summer grasslands on the other side of the mountains.

All along the Zagros Mountains the nomads seem to be lining up at a starting gate for a great race against time to reach summer food for the flocks and herds. Now there is no time for reciting ballads, telling old stories. Now everyone must prepare for the yearly migration. Tents must be struck and packed; animals must be rounded up and herdsmen appointed for the difficult journey. From the north to the south the Kurds, the Lurs, the Bakhtiari, the Kuhgelu, and the Khamseh Arabs line up along the mountains.

This will not be an easy journey through a mountain pass. The animals must eat as they go—the two-hundred-mile trip will take six or seven weeks—so families are spread out along the entire distance to take advantage of every blade of grass. The Bakhtiari, fifty thousand people with half a million animals, will take the most difficult course straight toward Zardeh Kuh, called the Giant of the Mountains. They will cross from

Shushtar to near Isfahan, taking a route of incredible danger.

This is not a journey to be undertaken without strict discipline. In charge of each tribal group is an hereditary ruler. Before the journey begins the Ilkhani sits on a rug and listens to the tribe members bring their complaints to him. Armed men bring thieves bound and tied. Men who have disagreed about the ownership of cows or sheep or horses come to have their quarrels settled. The Ilkhani listens and passes judgment which no one questions.

These tribal rulers, or Khans, are not poor, uneducated men. They are often very wealthy. They keep their wives and children in palaces on the high grasslands. They themselves may have been educated in America, or England or Germany. They own town houses and whole villages as well as the grasslands their tribesmen live upon. Some of them own oil lands, though they despise the men that work in the industry. But when the migration is to be made in the spring and again in the fall they come to travel with their people and no job is too difficult for them to undertake, no river too hazardous for them to swim, no mountain too forbidding for them to scale. Each may have a personal bodyguard of tall, skillful marksmen, each may have a group of fifty personal servants; but for the length of the migration they are once again primitive nomads.

Food during the journey will be simple: black bread and yoghurt made daily from fresh milk added to the culture in a goatskin. Before the journey is begun the Khans feast in their silk-lined tents, candles burn in tall brass holders, and priceless Persian carpets are spread out upon the grass. The foods, of course, vary, but they may be chicken, roast mutton, toasted bread spread with green onion leaves, rice pilau seasoned with sumac, mint, and salt, walnuts and raisins crushed together to make a paste, bowls of cool fruit juice called *shar-bart,* nuts floating in date juice perfumed with attar of roses, soft rich sweets. There will be no time for feasting after the trek has begun.

All of the tribes will have similar experiences on the journey, but the Bakhtiari, since they have the most difficult route, will have all the adventures multiplied.

At first the trail is almost level. It leads east from Shushtar over desolate boulder-strewn country, through tumble-down villages where the dirty women and filthy children come out to watch the strangers moving east. They jangle their bracelets and anklets of tarnished coins, but the tribesmen plod on.

Whenever the tribe moves there is a set and unchangeable order. Most of the people have made the trip so many times that they know what is expected of them and exactly where they belong in the moving mass.

First go the tribal rulers and their families. Though the Khans' wives and families usually are left the year around in a city near the summer grasslands, the Ilkhani may have brought along his sons or nephews to teach them the responsibility of the ruler in the semi-annual move from grassland to grassland. Next come the blooded horses. Next, the pack animals, and finally the herds driven by poor men, their wives, and their daughters. Children and young animals are often lashed to the top of the loads carried by donkeys, camels, or cows. For it is spring and there are babies everywhere: baby dogs, baby sheep, calves, and human babies, too old to ride in the wooden cradles lashed to their mothers' backs, yet too young to walk.

It is the women who have the hardest role in this trek. They are expected to assist in driving the family herds even though they carry a full-sized wooden cradle lashed to their backs.

If a woman allows an animal to stray, her husband can beat her and no one interferes. She is expected to be absolutely true to her husband. Polygamy has almost disappeared, but still the nomad's wife is looked upon as a possession.

The women are not veiled; but they are not dressed for mountain climbing. They wear a chemise-like blouse, long-sleeved and falling loosely to the hips. Over this they wear a sleeveless vest. Their skirts are long—almost to the ankle—and very, very full. Every step a woman takes, she must kick this heavy skirt before her. When it grows damp and soggy it wraps itself around her raw red ankles. Under the skirt she wears straight black trousers. Generally she is barefooted, but sometimes she wears shoes of white material—not leather. Her jet-black hair is braided into two braids which are brought to the front and fastened under the chin. Ordinarily these women have thin lips and humorless faces. It is their eyes that speak of beauty and dreams and love of life.

Who are these people who attempt this difficult journey without protest? No one knows. Their origin is a mystery, but many scholars think that they are the original Persians, their blood unmixed with the waves of invaders because of their way of life and rules of their tribes.

The first problem of the many Bakhtiari tribes making the journey is to cross a rushing spring-swollen river called the Kraun. The Kraun is half a mile wide and filled with whirl-pools and treacherous currents and rapids. There are no bridges, there are no boats. Still five thousand people carry with them everything they own in the world, and drive before them fifty thousand animals.

The men unpack the goatskins they have been carrying. They blow up several of these skins into tough balloons, and lash them together on a framework of sticks. This makes the raft that will carry the people across the river and on which the goats, who will not swim, will ride.

The tribal leaders know this river. They know the treacherous current and plan to use it. The current hits the western shore with great force. The raft is launched on this current and the rebound from the shore carries it downstream to the eastern shore. The raft with its boatman is launched again and returned to the west side of the river, where it is carried along the shore to the original launching point. Again and again the raft makes the same precarious trip. Meanwhile men, supported on blown-up goatskins, drive the herds unwillingly through the river.

It takes five days to put five thousand people on the eastern side. There is no time to worry about the sheep or cattle that have been drowned. There is not even time to mourn over the men who have been swept to their death in the swift current. Strangely enough there is much shouting and jesting and laughter. The trip still has the feeling of a holiday.

From the river the mountain rises abruptly and the climb begins. Much of the journey is made in the cool hours of the morning. On the eastern side of the first range of mountains is a long valley. Families are spread from one end of the valley to the other so that the herds will have good grazing. The people camp in circles around their animals to protect them from thieves.

The tribe moves slowly across the valley toward the next range of mountains. Herds must have time to make the most of the green pastures. While the animals graze the men cut grass and arrange it in packs. It must feed the animals during a forced march of two or three days over the grassless mountain.

During the stay in this valley the fine horses are driven to a mountain pass where there is less danger in crossing. The families of the Khans also take this safer route. But for the rest of the tribe no danger is too great. The second range of mountains is more formidable than the first, as it can be crossed only by making a zigzag trail across the face of the precipitous mountain. If anyone stops on this trail all must stop. There is no room to pass, no place to rest. At the summit where breaking a zigzag path is no longer possible, selected men clamber to the top and let down ropes so that everything can be dragged up and over.

Finally, after six weeks of camping in the long valleys and battling range after range of mountains, Zardeh Kuh is reached—the greatest obstruction of all. Here the virgin snow lies thick and as hard as ice. Slowly, painfully, the lead men dig a zigzag path, the Ilkhani himself directing the work. The snow they remove they pack on the outside of the track to serve as a protective wall. There are deep holes in the ice that must be avoided. Sometimes stubborn animals refuse to keep to the path and slide downward with almost human cries.

When the snow is hard the people put on their shoes. When the snow is soft they carry their shoes and plow through the frozen slush barefoot. The shoes would be spoiled by the wet.

And even when Zardeh Kuh is conquered the journey is not finished. The old, the young, the sick are strapped, facing backwards, onto donkeys and cows, and the journey down to the grasslands is begun. Slogging mile after mile in knee-deep snow the nomads travel toward the gorge that opens onto the high plateau. Here is grass. Miles and miles of grass. Here is sardsir, summer lands.

And all up and down the thousand-mile stretch of the Zagros range this same story is re-enacted with each of the tribes. On the upper grasslands the herds will fatten and the people will live their day-to-day lives until a breath of autumn is felt; then there will be another shivering of the Zagros and the two million nomads will again be on the march, this time retracing their way to *garmsir*—winter lands.

In this great drama of Grass each tribesman plays his part; the leading roles are certainly carried by the Khans who rule these people with a sort of benevolent despotism, keeping them in ignorance, allowing them to remain in poverty, yet dispensing justice with a quick and heavy hand so that the nomads, traveling though they are, feel a stability in their environment.

These tribal rulers who can command the absolute obedience of the tribesmen have made a very special problem for Iran. The loyalty of the nomad is for the tribe, not for the nation. All during the long history of the country, tribal Khans have grown strong and reached beyond the limits of the tribe and finally made themselves Shahs and Shah-an-Shahs, or King of Kings. This has been the basis for the changes in dynasty over the long years. The time has not passed when some other tribal ruler may accomplish this same feat again.

In 1909 it was the tribes that marched on Isfahan, captured it, then turned to Teheran and overthrew the Shah, demanding constitutional government.

When Reza gained power he knew that his greatest obstacle to holding that power would be the tribes. As soon as he became minister of war he started to disarm the tribesmen. The Lurs tribe would not give up its arms. Instead they started a war. And the Lurs were not the only ones that objected to being disarmed. Bakhtiari tribesmen ambushed a regiment of Cossacks, looted the survivors of guns and horses, and sent them back with the message, "The Bakhtiari are free!"

Reza did not let things rest. He pushed the campaign to

weaken the tribes through relocating the tribesmen in villages away from their tribal rulers. He took the Khans virtual prisoners and kept them in cities where they lived in luxury but lost touch with their people. But none of these methods really worked. Still the tribesman demands freedom. Always the kettle is boiling and the lid dances with the escaping steam.

Recently the attempt to relocate the tribes has been carried on with new vigor. On the plains of Dasht-i-Mogan, a fertile land just across the Russian border, for example, tribesmen have been given individual holdings which they can pay for over a long period of time. This land is fertile, lying between a river and a canal, and it should be possible to earn a fair living from the soil. Social workers and technical experts are ready to help the nomad-turned-farmer to settle into agricultural life. Permanent homes have been built for many of the families, and it is hoped that only the shepherds will move with the flocks, leaving women, children, and older men to take care of the farms.

On the border of Afghanistan similar attempts are being made. Who knows whether or not these efforts will succeed?

It is hard to understand the nomads of Iran, but without attempting to understand them we cannot realize just what the problems of Iran are, just what the resources in hardy men will be if ever the tribes give themselves with loyalty to Iran.

The problem is complicated by the fact that each tribe speaks its own dialect. The Kurds, Lurs, and Bakhtiari speak a language related to old Persian—an Indo-European language. The Arab tribes north of the Persian Gulf speak an Arabic dialect. The Shah Savans speak Turkish and the Baluchi of southeastern Iran speak still another dialect of Persian.

But the big difficulty is that the nomads love their lives. They are unhappy in villages even if new irrigation projects

**Workers on the "Road of Hope" make bread from the flour they have earned.**

should make enough tillable land available. The wild blood sings through the veins of the Iranian nomad. He endures hardships that civilized, cultivated men could not face, and in return for this he wants only to be free.

In 1953 a higher tribal council was formed to consider the health and education of these people, to consider ways to bring them into national unity. Each year the government continues its efforts, but still some of the tribes are in revolt. This very generation may make the last migration; this generation may see the last tents on the border.

# Twelve

# THE PEOPLE
# AND THE SOIL

THE MOUNTAINS and the deserts cover so much of Iran that only one-third of the land is suitable for forests, grazing land, and farms; yet almost seventy per cent of the people live outside the cities. Two-thirds of these people are farmers who live in villages and follow the quiet agricultural lives of their ancestors.

In the Caspian area neat houses stand in the midst of cultivated fields, but almost everywhere else in Iran the mud cottages of the farmers huddle together in squalid villages. The average number of people in a village is 345, but the median village has 164 people living in it. There are about 45,500 of these villages in Iran. Sometimes, where there is enough water and the soil is fertile, the villages are close together, probably a mile or two apart. Sometimes the village is isolated, a long way from other villages, even from connecting roads.

Through the center of most villages runs the *jube* (stream) that furnishes water for the village and for the fields and gardens around it. Anywhere along its course water is dipped into

Goats are driven down the main street in a village. Notice the women washing in the jube, the wall of mud-brick, and the thatched top that protects it.

great jars for daily cooking and drinking. The *jube* is the center of village life. Along it may run a short business street. There may be shops for selling tea, sugar, kerosene, naphtha, cotton yardage; a tea house, an apothecary shop, a mosque, a school, and a bath house. These buildings may be as primitive as the cottages of the villagers.

The village builders utilize native materials, bricks made of sun-dried clay—a very fine clay for this purpose is readily available in Iran—so the houses are the same color as the earth upon which they rest. The native contractors have a special way of building the walls so that they won't break down. At intervals the workmen build an added thickness, forming a sort of vertical buttress. The niches between these supports are on the inside of the house, and serve as storage space for folded bedding in the daytime. In the better houses a cupboard may be built into such a niche and on the shelves there may be brass cooking utensils, ornamental plates, and other treasures.

The roofs of the houses vary from one section of Iran to another. Where wood is available the houses have flat roofs with hewn beams. Over these beams branches are interlaced, and finally rushes or willows top the whole. The surface is dirt, rolled smooth with a roller which is kept on the roof for that purpose.

In areas where there are no trees the roof is made of the same brick as the house and is conical in shape like the igloo of the Eskimo. Here, too, the native builder has special ways to strengthen the walls and the roofs.

Each house, no matter how small, has a courtyard, walled with mud brick. Here the women do their cooking, the family

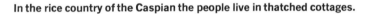

In the rice country of the Caspian the people live in thatched cottages.

**Gholam Hossein Chubackzan's wife, mother, and daughter meet him with excitement when he arrives home with the food.**

keeps its animals—oxen, a donkey, sheep, a dog, sometimes a cow, chickens—and if there is a latrine it occupies a corner.

Sometimes there is just one room in the cottage. The *kad-khoda* or headman of the village may have four. He is the representative of the landlord and must have room for an office. He is a combination overseer and mayor and is respected in the village.

No matter what the size of the house the housewife faces the same problems. With walls and floor of earth it is almost impossible to keep the place free of vermin. Since there are seldom glass windows, the house is always dark when the open doorway must be covered to keep out the cold.

The huts are heated in the winter with a *korsi*, a small fire built in the middle of a room, sometimes in a brass bowl. The fuel is dried animal dung or charcoal, though now it is unlawful to convert wood into charcoal. Over this tiny fire there is a stool, and spread over the stool and reaching to the floor on all sides is a *jajeem* (blanket). This little fire cannot warm an entire room. To get really comfortable one must sit near the *korsi*—the feet and legs, even the body, under the blanket. Sometimes there is tragedy with this *korsi*. Children may toddle into it, pushing aside the blanket and stool, and be severely burned.

These ugly houses face onto narrow, winding alleys, sometimes filled with refuse, always dirty and dusty. There is seldom a blade of grass, or a flower, or any growing thing.

Seen from a viaduct this Caspian city is crisscrossed with electric wires. Notice the western clothing of the men, the traditional *chadors* of the women.

In the old days, perhaps for protection, the village was surrounded with a sturdy wall. Sometimes the wall was of field stone, sometimes of mud bricks. Now many of these walls have crumbled, but still the houses huddle together.

Around the village spread the fields. Everywhere, except in the Caspian area, wheat is grown. Many of the villagers believe that wheat would poison them since they have never eaten any grain but rice. The fields also produce maize, potatoes, millet, peas, beans, and lentils. In the gardens there are cabbages, turnips, onions, eggplant, cucumbers and melons—especially cucumbers which the Iranians eat when they are very small and tender, and melons for which Iran is famous. An ancient crop was the opium poppy, which is now outlawed by the government. Now sugar beets, cotton, and tobacco are taking the place of the poppy.

There are no more beautiful orchards in all of the world than those in Iran's higher valleys. There are grown peaches—which originated in Iran, apricots—the quantity crop, plums, cherries, pears, pomegranates, and apples. Near the Caspian, subtropical fruits grow, and inland from the persian Gulf the people raise dates and eat them instead of bread. Olives grow on the southern slopes of the Elburz mountains, and all over Iran there are nut trees and mulberry trees.

For hundreds of years whole villages were owned by a single person. A man's wealth was not counted in dollars but in villages. Some men owned five villages—some a hundred. In those days earnings were often divided by the "rule of five": one for the landlord, one for the ox, one for the seed, one for the water, and one for the farmer. Since the landlord often owned the ox and water and furnished the seed, the farmer's share was one-fifth of the crop he produced. Today a landlord can own no more than one village. Other farming land is divided into ten-acre pieces and is farmer-owned.

The soil has become accustomed to the farmer's methods, which have scarcely changed in the last three thousand years. The oxen still pull a plow made of a forked tree limb, the plowshare encased in iron. The farmer still sows and weeds and cultivates by hand. He still cuts his grain with a sickle or scythe and ties it into sheaves and, as in Bible times, leaves some to be gleaned by those even more unfortunate than he.

In most places the threshing is done right in the fields, but some villages have a special threshing floor of hard-baked clay. The grain is piled on a cleared place in the field or upon the threshing floor and over it oxen pull a heavy frame with pro-

**Bread is made from CARE flour.**

jecting teeth. The grain is then kept until a strong wind arises, when a powerful youth tosses it into the wind so that the chaff is blown away.

Some of this grain will be coarse-ground right in the village and the farmer and his family will feast on fresh bread. Some will be packed on the backs of donkeys and carried in to the next town. Most will be hauled away by government trucks to be stored in great silos.

Since there is seldom enough water to irrigate all of the land, the farmer saves his soil by letting it lie fallow every other year. Some of the farmers have learned crop rotation and some plant the valuable alfalfa. Little use is made of chemical fertilizers; gardens are enriched with manure. As in the Far East, "night soil" or human excrement is used, which makes the vegetables and berries unfit for the consumption of strangers who have not grown used to foods grown in this way. One of the most peculiar fertilizers is pigeon droppings. Near Isfahan there is a great circular tower with hundreds of compartments for pigeons where the droppings are accumulated.

In the northeast and northwest portions of Iran the land is *daymi* (unirrigated). Elsewhere the land is *abi* (irrigated). For irrigation the qanat system is of more value than great dams and open canals.

Many of the village farmers are friendly and hospitable, but they are suspicious of the new and they fear foreigners and government agents. There is little laziness. Sometimes when a man is overburdened with debt he gives up and joins the professional beggars in the large cities.

The usual dress of the farmer is not too different from that of any other poor farmer. The men wear loose trousers and jackets. The women wear full long skirts, jackets much like blouses, and sometimes sleeveless vests made of sheepskin with the fleece inside. Dress for weddings and other ceremonial occasions may be quite elaborate. Each Persian village has its own native costume. In Sarbandan, a mountain village east of Teheran, the woman's costume starts with a sturdy pair of trousers made of satin or cotton which fit much like a too-large pair of American slacks. Over these is worn a tutu— the short full skirt of a dancer. Once a Persian monarch visited France where he was so enamored of the dancers that when he returned home he ordered the women of Persia to wear the tutu—over their regular trousers, of course. Over the trousers and the tutu is worn an overblouse, frequently tied

**Woman in traditional harem costume. The head-dress is Kurdish.**

with a narrow sash just below the breasts. The women love jewelry, especially necklaces and bracelets, and they like to tie pierced coins to the ends of their long black hair.

The food of the farmer is simple. He eats wheat or rice, a few vegetables in season, a little mutton, milk and yoghurt. Like all Iranians he likes sugar, and the amount of it in his sugar bowl is an indication of his prosperity and status. He must have tea. The Iranians use fourteen thousand tons of tea a year; of this they raise only seven thousand tons.

At the close of their yearly religious fast, at their weddings, on the eve of Mohammed's birthday, and especially at New Year's, even the poorest family must feast.

The favorite pastime, especially in winter, is listening to the telling of stories. Sometimes a traveling dervish comes through the village and recites long sections from the *Shahnama* or from the Koran in return for food and a place under the *jajeem*. In some families the ancient grandfather is the story-teller. It is amazing how much these men who have never learned to read can remember from Ferdousi.

The little girls play with dolls made from a bit of rolled-up rag. The boys roll up rags, too, to make a ball for their favorite game of soccer. Younger boys play a sort of marble game with date pits—or, now that Coke has come to Iran, with bottle tops. Another game is played with a matchbox. A matchbox is tossed by each boy in turn. If the box stands on end the thrower is king. If it lands on its side, standing on the narrower surface, the thrower is minister. The widest surface means that the thrower is a "thief" and must follow the orders of the king. The king may shout, "Around the village you run!" and the minister must see that the order is executed.

The game most loved by men and boys is *Alak do lak*. How old this game is, nobody knows, but Iranian men and boys have been playing it for centuries. The game is played with a bat, much like a baseball bat in thickness and length, and a short piece of wood, six or seven inches in length. The short stick is lifted into the air and struck with the bat. The players in the field try to catch the flying stick. The game is very rough—the flying stick may strike a player on the shin and cause temporary pain, or it may strike him in the face and put out an eye.

Hunting is a popular sport in Iran. The wealthy hunt the tiger, the brown bear, the panther, the jackal, the wolf, the fox, the wild sheep, the gazelle, the wild ass, and the pig. For the poor there are the hare and the game bird. The villager hides under a bright quilt until a curious quail alights on it, then reaches out and captures it.

There is a close family feeling everywhere in Iran. Families draw together to rejoice over a wedding, mourn a bereavement, or celebrate a homecoming. The villagers love to visit, the women in the home, the courtyard, or by the *jube;* the men in the tea house. The mosque and its religious ceremonies furnish the high points of the villager's year, but the center of the social life is the village bath.

Nearly every village has a public bath, with days for the women and days for the men. Women go into the bath, remove their clothing, and sit on trays placed on the ledge that runs around the bathing room. The ledge is made of a concrete-like material called *saruj* which has been in use in Iran for more than two thousand years. They rub themselves with soap or oil or with a kind of herb that produces a lather. They may pay a cabbage, a measure of grain, or a block of sugar to a bath attendant who will gently massage the tired body. After the massage the women dip into the public pool. All day the women talk and laugh and relax.

Because the seldom-drained, unchlorinated pools may be the source of contagion, showers are in some places taking the place of these village social centers.

For some time the government has been concerned about the low life-expectancy in Iran. Almost half the people are under twenty, which is proof of a high birth rate and a low life-expectancy. To lower the death rate the government and other agencies have attempted not only to establish clinics in many of the villages but to teach the people the rudiments of health and sanitation.

Village people find it hard to realize that the sparkling *jube* is filled with invisible danger. They fight against adding per-chlorine to their household water supply, and often object to bathing their dead, their dishes, their clothing and their children anywhere except on the banks of the stream.

Many villagers do not know the use of the latrine. The women and children use any field and the men turn toward any wall. The village version of a latrine is a three-walled building with one corner left open. There is no roof. Inside there is an open sewage well where flies buzz and breed. There is now a sanitation school in Iran where village people may learn, among other things, how to place a sanitary latrine slab over the pit, covering it except for an inverted bowl which is easily cleaned with the water from the *aftabe* (a large jar of water kept for cleansing purposes).

No one can guess when the farmer will give up the use of "night soil" in the cultivation of his garden; but the government is helping him learn the use of other fertilizers, to rotate his crops and to use other Western methods.

The government has been concerned, too, about illiteracy, especially in the villages. One of the first steps toward improving education was the abolishing of the *maktab,* a religious school where the scholars learned the Koran in Arabic. The government's aim, a school in every village, has not yet been realized. In some villages the schools have two grades, in some four, in some even ten. Schools for girls are less popular than schools for boys, but even in the villages many girls are learning to read and write while they receive instruction in sanitation and hygiene.

The greatest problem of the villagers in Iran is that of land ownership. In 1950 the Shah began to distribute his family holdings to the farmers who worked the land. He sold parcels for twenty per cent less than their actual value and gave each purchaser twenty-five years to complete the payment. This made the annual payment much less than the landlord's share had been when the soil was farmed on shares. The Shah did not add this money to his own account. Instead he invested it in necessary equipment, employed technical advisors, provided financial aid where it was necessary, and developed such community projects as schools, medical centers, and farmer cooperatives.

The farmer left alone with his new ten acres would have been in real trouble. He knew how to plow, how to plant, how to cultivate, how to irrigate, how to harvest. But where would he get seeds to plant and oxen to help him with the plowing and cultivating, water for irrigation? Now that all of the landlords are being forced to sell the land to the farmers, these problems have been pyramiding. The government of Iran has been doing all that it can to meet and solve them. Iran is rich in oil lands, and much of the money that comes from the oil is being spent for land reform and for agriculture.

Of course the program must go forward slowly. The farmer must learn to carry his new responsibilities; the development bank and the agencies that work directly with the farmer must work above graft and favoritism.

Yet real progress has been made, and the farmer, plowing a deep straight furrow toward the towering mountains, can look forward with confidence to the dignity of land ownership and a longer and better life for himself and his family.

**Farming methods are being changed in Iran.**

*Thirteen*

# IRAN'S CITIES

First Paragraph 12

THE IRANIANS are very proud of their cities. Five million people live in cities or towns, half of these in Teheran, Tabriz, Isfahan, Meshed, and Abadan. Other city dwellers live in one hundred three towns.

But few strangers share the Iranians' feeling for their cities. The first thing that a stranger sees is what seems to be endless walls, walls so high that only the tops of trees show above them. Everywhere is the same color—a pinkish drab of the desert carried into the city in bricks and building stones. Instead of the continuous glass front of the modern city's shopping district, one sees a series of small shops—some of them very beautiful indeed but many of them nothing more than holes in the ever-present wall with garish displays extending out onto the sidewalks.

The cities are built low, except for new structures, so they do not have the appealing skyline of New York City, or Istanbul.

Reza the Great cut wide streets through the cities. (In Shi-

**Modern buildings in Shiraz. Many beautiful buildings are a combination of the old and the new.**

raz the cutting of such a street destroyed an ancient mosque. In Isfahan the new asphalt strip dissected an ancient garden.) Without these wide streets city traffic would be impossible. Down them, especially in Teheran, pour thousands of cars imported from Italy, France, Germany, Russia, and the United States. Generally the cars move with such mad speed that identification is impossible.

Tourists are told that any Iranian who wishes to go into the taxi business can paint the fenders of his car white so it can be recognized at once as a cab, and he is in business. Often it seems that a two-decker bus, a taxi, a private car, a herd of sheep and a pedestrian are all moving toward the same open space with the intent to fill it. The drivers seem mad, absolutely mad, but somehow most rides turn out all right.

There are numerous well-kept squares or circles in Teheran, but these are scarcely visible for the traffic. Crowds of people move along the streets. The men wear Western clothes, as do some of the women. Near the government office buildings the girls click to work on high heels dressed in the latest and most tasteful Western costumes, but elsewhere in the city the women wear the long *chador* or veil, which is usually black but sometimes of a light print cotton. It is quite a trick to clutch this *chador* about oneself while clinging to the hands of a brood of children and carrying packages besides, but the women do it in all of the cities.

The stranger has just decided that Iranian cities are de-

A broad, modern street in Shiraz. Note the American tourist.

pressing, fearsome, and ugly when his impressions begin to change. He realizes that each city has three faces: *the old, the new* and *the ancient.*

It is *the old* that is ugly—the eternal walls, the jumble of architecture from every country that once held special privileges in Iran. But inside the walls there is beauty. Ring the bell at the narrow arched gateway of the courtyard; be admitted by a fresh-cheeked young houseboy, or a doddering old man, and you may be in a breathtakingly beautiful garden. The Persians, like the Japanese, love flowers and trees, pools and running water. Pass through the garden into the house where you are greeted by a charming hostess who speaks not only her own language but English and French as well. Here there will be Persian carpets of such beauty that the colors glow in the subdued light like jewels and the design is as intricate as those on the finest Persian silk. There will be art objects, each a museum piece, but all will be blended in such exquisite taste that none will challenge attention.

Many of the fine houses, hidden behind walls, have the kitchen across the courtyard from the rest of the house so that when dinner is served it has not been heralded by smells from the cooking area.

The famous Gulistan Palace where on No-Ruz the Shah holds *Salaam,* and where tourists are welcome most of the time, is also surrounded by a wall. The wall is monotonous on the outside, but on the inside it is decorated with glazed tile and encloses a garden of especial beauty. Part of the garden that surrounds the Marble Palace and the palaces that house the royal families is now enclosed by an iron fence so that the garden can be seen by passers-by.

*The new* is growing rapidly, especially in Teheran. A beautiful airport, luxury hotels, fine apartments have been built.

In Shimron, eight miles north of the city but really a part of it, there are many beautiful homes. Every day new suburbs are opening, and the multi-colored houses give a garden freshness to the arid land on which they are built.

In even sharper contrast are the old and new of Abadan. Braim is the area of company housing in this great oil city. Here there are green hedges instead of walls. The houses, set back from the road instead of fronting on it in the old manner, are surrounded by gardens and shaded by tall trees. The whole feeling is one of quiet and peace and withdrawal from the busy world. Just across the river is the old town with its noisy,

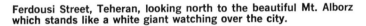

Ferdousi Street, Teheran, looking north to the beautiful Mt. Alborz which stands like a white giant watching over the city.

gaudy bazaar, with crowds of people, carts, bicycles, donkeys, and taxis with raucous horns. Colorful laundry hangs from every veranda and window. The whole feeling is one of movement and noise.

In nearly all of Iran's cities there is this contrast between the old and the new. Just as it is difficult to get used to seeing a herd of henna-decorated sheep being driven down an avenue where Imperials, Cadillacs, and fine European cars are parked, so it is hard to realize that the old and the new in architecture can snuggle so closely together. The public buildings in Teheran are as beautiful as any in the world. Especially the fine Senate building is an example of what Modern Iran will be when its building program is completed.

And then there is the *ancient face* of the cities. And here Iranian cities are truly the most beautiful in the world. The "three-day tourist" seldom reaches Isfahan, which is still "half the world" as it was in the days of Shah Abbas—that is in beauty alone. But one must close his eyes to the wretched hovels that still house many of the people and look at the ancient face—the brilliant aquamarine mosaic domes, the slender, heart-lifting minarets, the palaces, the mosques, the bridges. Isfahan is certainly the jewel of the Middle East.

Yet Isfahan is not the only city to show an indescribably beautiful ancient face. In Meshed, the holiest city of Shi'a Islam, is the shrine of Imam Reza. The golden dome over the actual tomb chamber is one of the most famous sights of the Islamic world. Besides the tomb there is a mosque of great beauty, the Old Court, the golden gate and minaret. Infrequently non-Moslems are allowed to visit this mosque, but always one can see the other mosques in the area and watch the devout Moslems making the great pilgrimage of their lives from all parts of Iran.

In Shiraz the tombs of Sa'di and Hafiz are built in the ancient manner, and Shiraz is the gateway to Persepolis thirty-five miles away.

What do city dwellers do for a living? In the old days—before Reza—most city dwellers were either merchants or government workers. The bazaars, the trading centers of the cities and towns, are still lively, noisy, and busy. In early times the farmers brought their produce to town and sold it in open fairs. Later a covered street was provided, and still later, spe-

A back street in Shiraz. Fifty years ago most commercial streets were like this.

cial bazaars were built. Sometimes the bazaar is a single street with small shops on each side. Sometimes several market-bordered streets run parallel with each other joined by intricate winding cross-streets. On each street one type of ware is shown. For example, there is a copper street, a jewelry street, a cotton-goods street, a leather street, a carpet street. The purchaser may look at the goods as long as he desires, and if he finds something he wishes to buy lively "trading" begins. From Bushir on the Gulf Coast in the south to the Caspian cities on the north, the people of Iran love a bargain and they go to the bazaar to find it.

"Five dollars, lady. Five dollars."

"Too much."

"For you, lady, I make it four dollars and sixty cents."

"Four dollars and sixty cents for that? Nonsense."

"Four dollars. My beautiful lady, this will be beautiful for you. You will honor this necklace by placing it on your neck. Four dollars."

"Four dollars? Too much. Come," she says to her friend, "let us find another jeweler who has better prices."

"Three dollars, my lady. . . ."

And so the bargaining goes on.

The bazaars are noisy, exciting, stimulating places to visit. A wife must not hold on to her husband's arm as they walk through the bazaar. This is considered vulgar.

Sometimes merchants do not hire a space in the bazaar. A seller of women's dresses, for example, may carry a dozen of them in a cloth-wrapped bundle. He puts the bundle down anywhere on the street and holds one dress at a time for passers-by to look at. Women actually buy dresses this way because they like the cut or the color, or think the material will be sturdy. These women will cover themselves with the *chador,* anyway. Women who dress in Western clothes usually select their patterns from *Vogue* or some other high-styled fashion book, and their material from specialty shops where excellent tailors make the costumes. There are few high-styled "ready-to-wears" available even in Teheran.

The dress merchant is not the only merchant on the street. A man, selling women "stretch" panties, puts both hands inside a small item and holds it high showing how great the stretch before the cloth gives way.

In Ghom, a religious center especially convenient for Moslem pilgrims, food is the chief item for sale. Merchants of green vegetables set up their stalls just outside the great mosque. They keep the vegetables fresh by dousing them every few minutes with water scooped from the passing *jube.* They carefully trim each head of lettuce or cabbage, and pilgrims, sitting along the streets, munch on the discarded leaves, gutter water and all.

But the merchants in the bazaars and those in the street stalls and on sidewalks are not the only merchants. There are big import-export businesses. Sometimes the headquarters of these businesses are in the bazaar area set in the midst of open courtyards away from the channel of the busy street. By far the most important article of trade is the world-famous Persian carpet. Carpets that will cover the luxury floors of the world are made by hand in Iran and sold through these exporters. Yet economists say that business in Iran has scarcely passed the bazaar stage.

Many of the city dwellers work for the government. An Iranian friend, speaking of a mutual acquaintance in America, said, "Ben is well educated. Why doesn't he work for the government?" This illustrates the ambition of many Iranians who attend school in America, in Europe, or in the excellent universities and colleges of Iran. Government employees range from agricultural and social workers who live and work in the villages, sometimes on the wild borders of the country, to the smartly dressed young men and women who are housed in modern, air-cooled offices. All are helping to modernize Iran and bring it abreast of the Western world.

But the greatest source of income for city dwellers is, of course, Industry.

A Teheran Telephone Company operator.

# Fourteen

# OIL AND INDUSTRY

LONG, LONG AGO, in the Paleozoic and Mesozoic geological eras, enormous deposits of oil were embedded in the limestone and sandstone of Iran. This limestone, called Asmara, breaks and fragments easily. When earthquakes occurred and lifted the entire Iranian plateau, many breaks allowed the gas from the underground deposits to come to the surface. This gas was ignited, perhaps by lightning, and became ever-burning flames. It was over these natural fires that the Zoroastrians built their fire temples.

All through the history of Iran these oil beds rested undisturbed. In 1902 a foreigner, William Knox D'Arcy, was given a concession to explore and exploit southern Iran. If the Iranians themselves had begun this exploration instead of granting a concession, Iran's history would have been different.

Six years after the exploration was begun a rich oil field was discovered at Masjid-i-Sulaiman. This concession was later operated by the Anglo-Iranian Oil Company. The British government was the majority stockholder.

In 1909 Abadan was a hot, dusty island at the head of the Persian Gulf. A few fishermen lived there, a few date growers. One day a Mr. Davidson, a young marine engineer, pitched his white tent there. Eighteen months later there were hundreds of white tents and two thousand men had flocked to the island. The reason? Mr. Davidson had come to Abadan to build a port and an oil refinery to refine the oil from Masjid-i-Sulaiman. This is now the largest refinery in the world.

Masjid-i-Sulaiman is not the only oil field. All along a line which stretches one hundred and fifty miles in a southeastward direction, oil centers have been located: Haft Kel, Naft-i-Safid, Agha Jari, Gach Saran. There are minor fields, too, like Naft-i-Shah and Lali.

The first concession was making the British rich but leaving little for Iran. In 1933 the concession was renegotiated and limited to one hundred thousand square miles. This was more favorable to Iran, but it was still an unfortunate arrangement.

Yet it was a good thing that a single company was operating the wells rather than several individual operators. They were opened up on a unit basis. Each well was scientifically placed to get out the most oil at the lowest cost. Because of the nature of the Asmara rock the oil can flow freely through intercommunicating fissures so that one well can drain an immense area. There is a great internal pressure which forces the oil to the well head which makes recovery less expensive than in most parts of the world. And reserves are enormous, especially at Gach Saran.

When the oil is recovered it must be refined. Some oil is used in its crude form, but that is a very small part of the output of Iranian wells. From Masjid-i-Sulaiman, Haft Kel, Naft-i-Safid, and Gach Saran, oil goes by pipeline to the refineries at Abadan. Oil from some other areas is shipped by tanker, and a great pipe line to Teheran was opened in 1957.

In 1944 two agents representing the oil companies of the United States and Dutch Shell went to Iran asking for concessions to explore and exploit in the east, and Russia at the same time demanded a concession covering two hundred sixteen thousand square miles. The Second World War was over, but Russia still kept her troops in the northern provinces of Iran. The Iranians said they would negotiate no concessions until all foreign troops had been withdrawn. Russia then used diplomatic threats and when these didn't work, strikes and demonstrations. These disturbances made a change in government. An old man, Dr. Mossadegh, had formed a national front party. The demand of this political party was that Iran should own and operate the oil fields and have the profits from these rich natural resources.

But Russia kept threatening. She said her troops would not be withdrawn unless she were given some oil concessions. The prime minister finally made a promise to present a plan to the Majlis. But the Iranians were tired of Russian interference. Iranian troops marched into the northern province of Azerbaijan and the Russians withdrew.

The continuing participation of the British in the oil profits worried the Iranians. They demanded nationalization, and in 1951 the prime minister, who opposed nationalization, was assassinated. With Dr. Mossadegh as the new prime minister, the oil industry was nationalized.

Now the production and refining of oil came to a dead stop. The Iranians did not know how to conduct the business, and the British made marketing almost impossible. Finally, in 1953, the problem was settled. An international consortium would produce and market Iranian oil and Iran would have at least half of the profits (in some cases seventy-five per cent).

Naft-i-Shah was excluded from this agreement. It is operated by National Iranian Oil Company and distributes its oil
within Iran.

Because Iran has this source of income the country has
been able to encourage other industries and carry out a program of general welfare. In Iran not the Shah, but a specially
appointed committee of experts called PLAN, in cooperation
with all government departments, decide how the money
should be spent.

PLAN's first interest is to encourage agriculture, since the
people must be fed, and since such a large part of the population depends upon farming. Its second interest has been communications, including, of course, the building of roads, the
extension of railroads, and the construction of airports as well
as the development of the services we ordinarily think of as
communication services.

The third interest has been industry. Never will the land be
able to support the people—although Iran does not have the
population problems of India, Pakistan, and some other un-
derdeveloped countries. Many of the people must work in
industry if a high standard of living is to be reached and main-
tained.

PLAN has made a careful study of the resources of the
country. Next to the oil resources may be the fishing resources.
The Caspian Sea is the largest producer of caviar in the world.
There are other fishes, too. On the gulf coast there are so
many varieties of fish that large canning industries could be
supported if private investment could be interested.

Since Iran has both coal and iron one would expect an important steel industry; but heavy industry is just beginning to
make a place for itself in the economy. For many years the
only heavy industry has been the production of cement prod-

ucts. Now that there is a great demand for automobiles, Iran has made a small beginning in this field. In 1959 the first assembly plant in Iran was inaugurated by the Shah. This assembly plant makes Willys Jeep vehicles including trucks and ambulances. As well as assembling imported parts, some parts are manufactured. Soon all of the parts may be made in Iran. In 1961 the Fiat Motor Company began to assemble Fiats, and now the German Mercedes-Benz Company is assembling trucks and buses.

Fish from the Caspian Sea. Persian caviar is the most famous in the world market.

It seems obvious that Iran should have developed a textile industry. The raw materials are produced, the people need fabrics, and the Iranian gift for textile design is as old as any of the ancient arts in which Iran has always excelled. In 1917 a spinning mill was built by private capital in Iran. In 1922 another private investor built spinning mills at Isfahan. The textile industry soon made Isfahan one of the busiest industrial centers of Iran. In 1932 Reza Shah turned his attention to textiles. During World War II imports of cotton goods were cut off and the spinning and weaving industry was stepped up to take care of the country's needs. But when the war was over, cheap goods from India and other neighboring countries flooded in and the industry ceased to grow. Now there is a concerted plan to build this industry. It will, of course, never equal the oil industry in either importance or income, but it will furnish less expensive cotton goods for the people who need it so much and give employment to many men and women.

The manufacture of vegetable oil, especially from cottonseed, has progressed rapidly, as has the manufacture of sugar. At one time Iran had a flourishing sugar industry built upon the production of cane. Now the industry depends upon sugar beets. In 1930 there were thirteen modern sugar refineries, but many more are planned for the near future. Iran still must import sugar since sugar, tea, and rice are the principal purchases of the people. There are fifty-eight modern tea processing plants, forty-nine more which need to be rehabilitated, and plans for further building. Iran produces only a third of the tea the people drink—for the people are great tea drinkers. Tea is served in every home, in shops while the customers are being served, in beauty parlors while the ladies rest under the dryers—everywhere.

One of the newest factories, between Teheran and Karaj, is a great plant for producing medicines. This one plant will produce eighty per cent of the medicine needed by the people of Iran. To watch the young women, dressed in white uniforms, busy at their intricate tasks, gives one the feeling of the new Iran, just as a trip to the bazaar gives one the feeling of old Iran.

About thirty miles west of Teheran is the Razi Serological Institute. This institution works primarily at making serums for animal diseases, but also carries out research on human diseases, and produces vaccines for anthrax, diphtheria, tetanus, and whooping cough. In December of 1959 the African Horse Sickness reached Iran from Pakistan and Afghanistan,

A modern factory near Teheran, a hint as to what tomorrow will bring.

carried by a minute sand fly. The Razi Institute went to work on the disease immediately, and isolated fifty separate strains. The problem with the disease was that there were just a few hours from the first symptom until the death of the animal. In one area two hundred thousand horses were affected in one week—a loss of $10,000,000. In four months the Razi Institute was providing vaccine for Iran, and by October the disease was wiped out and this Iranian institution was helping to fight it in Turkey, Syria, Cyprus, Afghanistan, and Pakistan.

A game that little boys once played with pebbles is now played with the caps from soft-drink bottles. "Pepsi" manufactured in Iran tastes just like its American counterpart. But the Iranians speak of "Canada" when they mean a bottled orange drink. In Iran, where the drinking water is unsafe except in the big cities, it is pleasant for tourists to be able to purchase bottled drinks manufactured under sanitary conditions. The Iranians love these drinks, too. In nearly every village that fronts the highway there is a soft-drink stand with violent-colored drinks displayed. The modern bottling plants look as if they had come on a magic carpet straight from America.

PLAN does not want the young people suddenly to leave the villages and flock to the cities to work in the factories. Members of PLAN know what happened during the industrial revolution in Western European countries. Iran's cities are not ready to absorb large numbers of people not oriented in the ways of city living. There would be social problems, sanitation problems, which add up to human problems. For this reason PLAN offers special concessions to investors who will start their plants away from Teheran.

Perhaps the most promising industrial movement is the interest in cottage industry. Carpets have always been made in

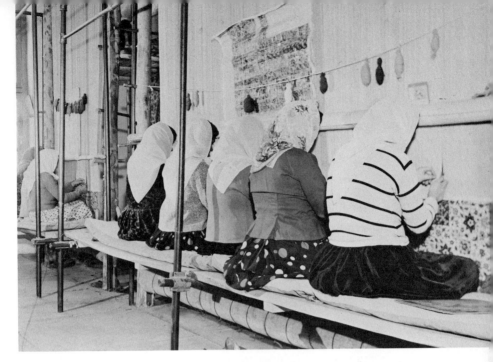

Modern carpet loom.

the home or tent. Now there is interest in producing other materials in small factories located in the villages. The women can keep their homes, rear their children, and still add to the family income. In these industries not the quantity of material produced, but the value in human dignity, must be considered.

Iran is proud of its beginning industries. It should be. It takes capital, executive ability, technical ability, cooperation to make industry profitable. These are not easily found in Iran.

In America everyone is accustomed to working with his hands. The manager of a large industrial plant may return from his office eager to spend an evening working on hand-made furniture; a bank president may hurry home to build his own hi-fi; a society woman may knit her own sweater or take pleasure in making ceramic objects for her own home.

In Iran work with the hands is left largely to servants. One does not see the mistress of a fine estate out digging up her own iris bulbs or setting in bedding plants. One never sees the government accountant mowing his own grass or setting cement in his own patio. And because there has always been a serving class, people grow up without what we call "American know-how." American university professors in such subjects as physics say that students from Iran and other countries of the Middle East and subcontinent are excellent at solving mental problems; but when it is necessary to invent and create instruments to further an experiment, they find themselves definitely at a loss. Their hands have not been educated.

Perhaps the industrialization of Iran which has now begun so bravely will help to create a new middle class—a class that honors physical work while still striving toward mental attainment.

# Fifteen

# TOMORROW IN IRAN

WHEN His Imperial Majesty, Mohammed Reza Shah Pahlavi, Shah-an-shah of Iran, was a thirteen-year-old schoolboy in Switzerland he dreamed a great dream—not the sort of dream that comes to one in the night and is forgotten by morning, but the sort of dream that is inspired by a great story and stays with the dreamer for months or even years. The boy, Mohammed Reza, was reading the story of his country and of the king who reigned fourteen hundred years ago. The great Anoushiravan attached a chain to his royal palace gate. Anyone seeking justice could pull the chain and a great bell would announce to the king that one of his subjects was in distress. The story said that once a donkey pulled the chain which rang the bell. The donkey had been mistreated by his owner. Because Anoushiravan cared about the welfare of his subjects there could be no injustice in Iran.

Mohammed Reza knew that in the country ruled over by his father such a chain and bell would be impractical. For a time he considered a distress-box arrangement. People who felt that they were treated unjustly could put in such a box a report of their troubles and the Shah could order investigation.

But as the boy grew older and was suddenly seated on his father's throne, he realized that Iran didn't need a chain and bell. It didn't need a distress-box. What Iran needed was a Shah who was sensitive to the needs of his people, other government officials who would conceive and carry out measures to lessen poverty, suffering, and injustice.

Almost from the first day of Mohammed Reza's reign he has been conscious of his country's problems and has warned leaders to prepare for an evolution from above rather than the usual revolution from below. In 1952 he proposed a program

His Imperial Majesty and Empress Farah greet Lyndon B. Johnson, then (1962) Vice-president of the United States, and Mrs. Johnson.

for reform based on six principles of social justice: housing, food, clothing, education, sanitation, and health. In 1961 the Shah dissolved the Parliament in order to facilitate his reform program. He ruled by decree with the advice and assistance of his ministers. In 1963 he called upon his people to vote for or against six laws which would drastically change Iranian life.

1. A land reform program which at the time of the referendum had already distributed farm lands to 52,112 peasant families.

2. Sale of government-owned factories to finance the land reform program.

3. A new election law to make the elections really democratic. (Rigged elections had been popular in the past.)

4. Nationalization of forests.

5. Formation of a corps of fifty thousand teachers to work in rural areas where the population is eighty per cent illiterate.

6. A plan to give workers twenty per cent of the net profits of factories. This does not include state-owned industries nor the Iranian Oil Company. Workers in these companies will receive bonuses.

Large land-owners, big businessmen, Moslem religious leaders, and one of the political parties were opposed to these measures. They combined with the extreme left wing to cause riots in the cities, especially in Teheran; the bazaars were closed and the people were asked to not go to the polls.

How firmly the people supported the Shah was shown when nearly all of the votes cast were for the measures. In Teheran there were 521,674 in favor of the measures and only 834 against them.

Perhaps the landlords and their associates had gone too far

in opposing the Shah's reforms, especially the land reforms. In Fars, where Cyrus founded the Persian Empire, there were 450 wealthy families who wanted no change. They gained the cooperation of the mullahs, who preached to the illiterate people and tried to frighten them. Then, as land reform continued in spite of their opposition, these conservatives evidently employed an assassin to murder the young land reform agent. Instead of helping their cause the murder set people against the land-holders. Agriculture Minister Hasan Arsanjani, who had pushed land reforms under two premiers, ordered the land distribution to be completed in forty-five days. The Shah said, "There is no longer any place for privileged landlords seeking prosperity from the privations of working peasants who have equal rights to happiness."

PLAN Organization says that reforms in Iran cannot come about in a day or a year or ten years. "It will take at least a generation to accomplish the far-reaching changes in attitudes and institutions and economic structure which continued development requires."

An evolution from above is not easy. There are people in Iran who are devoted to the Shah and willingly cooperate with every plan that he thinks is important. There are others who oppose him. Some of these feel that the Shah is not sincere in his efforts; others, like the landlords, lose their wealth and power when his plans begin to operate; still others feel that the Shah's rather slow-paced efforts are not enough and that revolution would be better. The result of the plebiscite show that the Shah's supporters far outnumber those who are against him.

Less than fifty years ago the women of Iran were wrapped in *chadors*. Their faces were covered when they were outside their homes and in their homes when strangers were present. Their place was in the home and for them no education except in household matters was considered necessary.

The first move in freeing the women was Reza Shah's proclamation requiring them to walk in the streets without their faces covered. He also demanded Western clothing, but anyone in Iran today can see that change of dress will come slowly. Many of the young office and government workers wear the latest European styles, but most Iranian women, young or old, cling to the chador.

Next came the increasing of educational opportunities. Now women work in nursing, school teaching, office positions, and in medicine, law, engineering and banking. Iranian women are professors, scientists, army officers, industrialists. Iran's minister of education is a woman as are six deputies and two senators in the parliament.

In the villages progress has been slower. One woman, scouring a brass pot at the village *jube*, was muttering to herself, "I work and work and nobody appreciates me." Another old woman was asked if she would take advantage of women's suffrage granted in 1963 and she said, "A woman does not need to vote. All she needs is the love of her husband and the respect of her children."

Young women do not agree with this old woman. They are eager to take jobs in factories; to attend the University of Teheran with the men. Soon the women of the villages will begin to take their place in society. Social workers are going into even remote villages to teach the women health, sanitation, good grooming, reading and writing. When all women have taken off the chador maybe they will feel new and different.

Many people feel that "black gold," the oil that brings

so much revenue into Iran (only the United States, Soviet Russia and Venezuela produce more), is at the basis of Iran's rapid progress. One has only to look at backward oil-rich countries to know there must be other causes. Stability, the government, the political situation and the desire of the people to move upward are all factors.

In 1963 the Shah introduced the "White Revolution." He is determined to show that great change can come by working within the establishment, starting from the top, probably greater change than can come from the streets.

Ten years ago Iran was receiving aid not only from the American government but from CARE, an organization using funds raised in the United States and Canada. The Iranian government has now informed the United States that Iran needs no more AID. In January, 1970, the Shah thanked CARE for the 23 million dollars spent there for schools, clinics, roads, rebuilding of earthquake-destroyed villages— all self help projects—but said that Iran could now take care of its own problems.

Since 1965 the annual income for each person has increased from $187 to $300. This is still pitifully small since an average family of four would have $1200 a year to live on; some having much more but most having much less.

Perhaps the reason for increase in income is the rise of new industries which means more jobs, more goods for the people, more material for export. Iran now produces automobiles, refrigerators, shoes, exportable textiles. Factory workers are made to feel "partners in business." In addition to salary each worker receives a share in the earnings. Profit sharing has increased production. Some heavy industry is already coming, including iron and steel mills and the production of petrochemicals.

Another cause for the advancement in per capita earnings has been land reform. This was the earliest reform begun by the Shah and he is determined that some day every man will till his own soil. The peasant's life has become better and richer, and two-thirds of the 28 million people in Iran are peasants. He feels pride in the work he does on his own land and joins village cooperatives which help him to buy and improve his seed and his stock and to sell his produce to good paying markets. With personal ownership, production has increased appreciably.

The great landowners who have lost their land are given an opportunity to buy shares in government-owned factories, making them eager for the success of industry.

All reforms depend upon the people's being ready for them —ready to accept them and ready to participate in them. For that reason education is the most pressing part of the reform program. During the reign of Reza the Great, students were sent to European universities for advanced study, a National Teachers' College was founded, and the University of Teheran was established. High schools were built and elementary schools became four times as numerous as before his coming to power.

Now there are free schools and attendance is supposed to be compulsory, but if every child attended school the present buildings would be completely inadequate.

After six years of elementary school the student moves into a three year intermediate school which corresponds to our junior high school. High school may emphasize academic or vocational education. The high school graduate may receive a degree in science or education by completing courses in one of the six departments of the Iranian Polytechnic Institute or he may attend university classes in Teheran,

**The Mathematician. Gohar School in Teheran.**

Shiraz, Isfahan, Tabriz, Ahwaz, or Meshed or in any of the more than fifty universities and colleges. Twenty thousand students now study in the United States or Europe.

Iran needs many more technical workers, and more bright students should take vocational training. The stigma of working with the hands should be forgotten.

The most innovative thing that Iran has done in education is the organization of the Educational Corps. Iran has universal draft of *all* high school graduates, but the young man or woman, drafted into service of his country, can choose his field or service. Nearly 60,000 young men and 4,500 young women have gone into the rural areas to battle against ignorance and illiteracy. The schools these young people teach in are open not only to children, but to their parents and grandparents, so everyone can learn to read and write.

Iran has attacked its sanitation and public health problems with energy. The Moslems are a clean people. They do not pray without washing themselves, and in the courtyards of the mosques there is always water available for ablutions. Yet such washing is not enough. To take the place of unsanitary public bath houses, new baths are being built in towns and villages. Even city dwellers with showers in their own homes prefer to take their children and their servants with them for a morning at the baths where there are not only showers available but experts to shampoo the hair and massage away the aches of tense muscles. Yet there are still remote villages where there are no baths, no latrines. Many people, especially nomads who have no fixed home, haven't learned their importance. Social workers are training women to want sanitary facilities. Development corps, made up of university and technical school graduates, are doing a magnificent job in

**Games at a Teheran girls' school.**

improving the sanitary conditions and the physical facilities of the villages.

There are thousands of people to each doctor in Iran. What makes the problem even greater is that most of the doctors prefer to live in the big cities. This leaves the people in remote areas with little medical attention. There are fine hospitals in cities—as fine as any hospitals in the world. The health corps, comprised of doctors and dentists, is carrying help to the villages and many of the village clinics offer excellent service.

Yet in the field of health there is still a long way to go. Some of the clinics are conducted by men who have completed only premedical training and have never had patients before they come to the clinic. Such a doctor if he is learning and improving is infinitely better than none. Midwives, who know nothing of the need for cleanliness, deliver most of the babies. These women need special training to reduce death in childbirth.

Perhaps the answer to many of these problems in the future will be the mobile health unit, but since so many villages are entirely away from usable roads the success of this method would depend upon improvement of communication between scattered villages.

The Shah and his government have made great strides toward preventative medicine and thousands of years of life have been given to the people through the presence of the right needle, the right serum, the right technician and the right educational preparation. The problem of low life expectancy has especially concerned the Shah, so Iran has been making real improvement in this field.

But the greatest battle of all is against poverty. In Iran two-thirds of the people are farmers, yet farms produce less than half of the gross national product, even with the growing success of land reforms. This means that if poverty is to be lessened, not only must farm methods be improved but there must be a large-scale movement out of agriculture and into other employment. Growing industry will continue to absorb much of this manpower, but the farm worker, ignorant of everything but how to plow and plant, must become an expert in some other field. Improved village education with some means of taking the most adaptable students from the village schools and giving them special education in vocational schools is helping to make this changeover.

The programs for education, health, and local improvement can absorb more workers. Those working in education, health, engineering, the sciences, will have to be highly educated men

Letters are written for those who cannot write themselves by this scribe who makes his office on the street in Teheran.

One of the thousands of workers who built schools and clinics in the Persian Gulf Coast area. These builders were paid with CARE food.

and women, but local improvement projects can absorb many. In September of 1962 when the Shah visited the district where villages had been almost wiped out by earthquake, he promised the people that Iran would undertake a great home building project. Mud houses with thick walls had collapsed with the shaking of the earth and had crushed the people. A more sophisticated type of building would be able to withstand earth tremors.

CARE delivered hundreds of tons of food, medical supplies and tents for temporary shelter. Next the organization studied the area and decided to spend $400,000 to reconstruct the town of Nuhum. Roads, homes, schools, markets, civic structures were built by 100 men who had survived the quake. Such home building projects can absorb both the skilled and unskilled laborer and at the same time improve living conditions.

Everything cannot be done in a day or a year. But the White Revolution is securing steady improvement in the standard of living, banishing the deepest poverty, increasing security against the main hazards of life and providing more equal opportunity. Iran is the fastest developing country in the world!

As Americans we can be proud of what our nation did to lend a hand-up when Iran needed help. Our government with its Point Four program, later with AID, gave not only financial assistance but technical advice. Private agencies have helped, too. The Near East Foundation did much to train Iranians to teach others in such fields as agriculture, sanitation and social service. America has had a part, too, in such international agencies as UNICEF.

From 1958 to 1963 there was a terrible famine along the Gulf Coast. There were no rains and grain could not mature.

The people tried to live on dates, but dates do not sustain life. The Red Lion and Sun, the Iranian Red Cross, saw the condition of the people. A gift of food was not enough. Food would keep people alive but it would not save morale. The Red Lion and Sun worked with CARE to make a wonderful plan of assistance.

They planned to build an all-weather road along the sand and rock crusted coast of the Persian Gulf, the *Road of Hope*. This would be the first modern transportation facility connecting the industrial provinces of the north with the dry, desolate Fars region. The road would connect Bushir and Lengeh, four hundred and fifty miles away. Feeder roads would run from this road back to the remote villages. Along this road trucks would bring fish from the gulf to the starving people. The government created an agency, called the Southern Ports and Isles Development Organization, to administer the program; the Red Lion and Sun provided warehouses and transported food inland for distribution; and CARE furnished the food from American surplus stores.

The road was not built with heavy machinery, but built with pick and shovel. Two thousand men could work on the road at one time. These workers would be men who were idle because they could not till their sunburned fields. Each man would work for two months and receive food for a family of nine for four months, after which other men would take their places on the road.

If you had been in one of the courtyards where the food was being paid to the workers—

If you had seen the payroll: Hasan, son of Amir; Ali, brother of Masood—for these Persians have no last names—

If you had seen the look of pride and happiness on the men's faces as they put their mark on the payroll and received

**Some of the men who built the road between Bushir and Lengeh.
They received their pay in food through CARE.**

their flour, shortening, and dried milk—

If you had read on each container, "This is a gift of the American people"—

You woud have turned away, unable to speak, with tears of pride and love in your eyes and throat. *I did.*

By the time CARE's agreement with the government had been completed in 1955, 30,000 Iranians and their families had been kept alive and hopeful with American food, 200 kilometers of road had been completed, new job opportunities had opened in the Fars region. There was increased activity in the deepwater ports, and marked increase in the wheat crop.

Now Iran does not need the help of outside agencies. With a strong and wise government, stable currency, and an emerging middle class, Iran is able to make its own future.

There is still a wide gap between rural and urban population, between rich and poor. There is still bribery and corruption in places. But these defects have taken centuries to grow. How can they be erased without decades of effort?

Surely, for Iran, tomorrow will be better.

**A worker leaves for home with the food he has earned.**

# Index

Abadan, 119, 123, 130
Abbas, Shah, 18, 69, 71-75
Abbassido, 55, 56
Aboubakr, 54
Abu Ali ibn Sina (*see* Avicenna)
Achaemenids, 21, 22, 25, 26, 28,
    30, 33, 40, 41, 48, 57, 91
Afghanistan, 78, 103, 136
Agriculture, 12, 18, 47-50, 80, 95,
    103, 105, 110-112, 116-118,
    132, 141, 149, 151
Ahasuerus, 26
Ahmad, Shah, 79, 80
Ahura Mazda, 28-30, 33, 46
Ahwaz, 147
AID, 152
Alexander the Great, 35-39
Al-Ghazali, 59
Ali, 54, 55, 68, 74, 88
Allah, 52
Alp Arslan, 57
Amayyad, 56
Amayyads, 55
America, 79, 127, 131, 147, 152-4
Anahita, Temple of, 42

Anglo-Iranian Oil Company, 129
Anoushiravan, 45, 46, 139
Antioch, Syria, 39
Apadana, 22-4
Arabia, 12, 23, 51, 54, 69, 103
Arbela, 36
Architecture, 23-25, 42, 46, 59-60
    64, 67, 69-71, 73, 75, 106-108,
    122, 124
Ardashir, 42, 43, 44, 46
Aristotle, 36, 64
Armenia, 41, 42, 43, 69, 73-4
Arsaces I, II, III, 40
Arsanjani, Hasan, 142
Arts and crafts, 19, 22, 25, 226,
    34, 39, 44, 47, 60, 64, 67, 75
Aryans, 11, 19
Asmara, 129, 130
"Asassins," 57, 61
Assurbanipal, 28
Assyrians, 19
Astyages, King, 20
Ataxerxes, 25
Athens, 21
Avesta, 41, 56

Avicenna, 56
Azerbaijan, 64, 68, 69, 73, 131

Babylon and Babylonia, 26, 38, 41
Bactria, 37, 40
Baghdad, 44, 56
Bahai, Sheikh, 74
Bahram IV, 45
Baluchi and Baluchistan, 85, 103
Banks and banking, 76, 78, 79
Battles: Arbela, 36, Marathon, 21,
    Nihavand, 54, Oxus River, 54,
    Qadisiyya, 54, Salamis, 21, 35
Baysunghur, 65
Bazaars, 126-127
Beshahr, 18
Belt, 18
Bible, 19, 26, 33
Bihzad, 67
Bokhara, 57
Bombay, 31, 32, 54
Books, 64, 65, 67
Bushir, 152

Calendars, 52, 57, 79, 89, 91
Cambyses, 20, 21
CARE, 152, 154
Carpets, 44, 92, 97, 122, 127, 136
Caspian Sea, 11, 12, 14, 16, 18,
    47, 77, 79, 105, 110, 132
Celebrations, 87, 88-94
Chador, 81, 83, 88, 121, 127, 144
Christians, 41, 52, 63
Chronicles of the Kings (see Shah-
    nama)
Commerce, 12, 62, 127
Communications, 35, 132, 149
Communism, 82
Costume, 24, 31, 83-85, 88, 99,
    112-114, 121, 126-127, 143
Croesus, King, 20
Ctesiphon, 44, 47, 54
Cyaxares, King, 19, 20
Cyprus, 136
Cyrus, 20, 21, 26, 34, 38

Damascus, 56
Dams, 58
Daniel, 26
Daqiqi, 56
Darab Shah, 35, 36
D'Arcy, William Knox, 129
Darius, 21, 22, 26, 27, 34, 35
Darius III, 36-38
Dasht-i-kavir, 16
Dasht-i-lut, 15, 16
Dasht-i-Mogan, 103
Davidson, Mr., 130
Day of Resurrection, Reckoning,
    52
Dervishes, 63, 68, 114
Deserts, 14-17
Dhalla, 28
Diseases, 135-136

Ecbatana, 19, 20, 21, 22, 36
Education, 57, 62, 67, 97, 104,
    116, 117, 138, 141, 143-147,
    151
Egypt, 22, 48, 61
Esther, 26

Family life, 83-84, 91-96, 107-
    109, 114, 115, 137-138
Famine, 152
Farid ad-din Attar, 59
Fars, 42, 64, 68, 142
Farvadin, 91
Fath' Ali Shah, 77
Ferdous, 16
Ferdousi, 11, 35, 36, 45, 56, 63,
    69, 91, 114
Firuzabad, 46
Fish and fishing, 14, 132
Fitzgerald, 59
Food and drink, 83-84, 86, 88,
    92-93, 95, 97-98, 110, 114, 127,
    134, 136, 152-154
France, 77, 113, 146
"Friends of the Shah," 72
Funeral customs, 31-32, 87-88

Gach Saran, 130
Games and sports, 45, 69, 114-115
Gardens, 122
Garmsir, 102
Gawhar Shad, 64-5
Genghis Khan, 61, 62
Genoa, 62
Geography, 12-17
Georgia, Russia, 64, 69, 77
Germany, 82
Ghazali, 56
Ghazan Khan, 62
Ghaznavids, 56
Ghazni, 56
Ghom, 127
Girehban, 31
Government and politics, 26, 34,
    40, 46, 54, 57, 78-81, 102-104,
    116-118, 131, 139-152
Great Britain, 74-75, 77-78, 82,
    129-131
Greece, 11, 21, 26, 33, 35, 36, 44
Gypsies, 45

Hafiz, 65-67, 125
Haft Kel, 130
Hamadan, 19, 68
Haram, 53, 64, 67, 91
Harpagus, 20
Hasan as-Sabbah, 57
Hashish, 57
Hassan, 55, 88
Health, 104, 116, 147-149
Herat, 65, 67
Herodotus, 20
Hindus, 28, 64
Hospitals, 62, 148
Hotu, 18
Houses and housing, 19, 62, 103,
    105-109, 122-123, 141, 151
Hulugu, 61-62
Hussein, 55, 88-9

Ilkhani, 97-8, 101
Imams, 55, 88-9

Imamzadehs, 55
India, 41, 44, 54, 64, 76, 134
Indo-Iranians, 19
Industry, 80, 128, 132-138, 141
Invasions, 19, 35-8, 54, 57, 61,
    64, 69
Iranian Oil Company, 141
Iranian Polytechnic Institute, 146
Iraq, 39, 68, 74
Irrigation, 14, 16, 47-50, 112
Isfahan, 14, 59, 69, 73, 97, 102,
    119, 120, 124, 134, 146
Islam, 33, 52 54 55, 57, 59, 62-
    65, 68, 86, 88, 91, 124, 127,
    141, 148
Isma'il Shah, 68, 69, 75, 77
Issus, 36
Istakhr, 42
Ivan, 42, 59, 70

Jajeem, 109, 114
Jami, 67
Jamshid, 91
Jerusalem, 26
Jews, 26, 33, 52, 69, 74
Jube, 49, 105-6, 115, 116, 127
Julfa, 73

Kadkhoda, 107
Karachi, 31, 32
Karaj, 135
Karim, Khan, 76
Kerman, 68, 77
Khans, 97-8, 101-3
Khorasan, 54, 64, 68, 69, 73
Khosrau I, 44, 45
Khosrau the Just, 46
King of Kings, 30, 33, 41, 92,
    102, 139
Koran, 52, 55, 64, 65, 86, 88, 89,
    93, 114, 117
Korsi, 108-9
Kushti, 31

Labor problems, 131
Lakes, 14-15
Lali, 130
Language, 19, 28, 41, 44, 103; Arabic, 55, 56, 103, 117; Babylonian, 26; Elamite, 26; English, 122; Old Persian, 26, 103; Pahlavi, 41, 56; proto-Elamite, 19; Turkish, 103
Laws, 19, 97, 141
Legends, 35-6, 38-39, 43, 45, 56, 69, 91
Literature, 35, 44, 56, 59, 62, 63, 66, 74, 89

Macedonia, 35, 36
Mahmud, 56, 57
Majlis, 78-9, 80, 131, 141, 144
Makruh, 53
Maktab, 117
Malek Shah, 57
Mandane, 20
Mani (Manichaeism), 46
Maragha, 64
Marathon, 21
Marriage customs, 85-87
Marvdasht, plains of, 22
Masjid-i-Sulaiman, 129, 130
Mathematicians, 57, 59
Mazanderan, 64, 80
Mecca, 52, 53, 74, 86
Medes, 11, 19, 20, 23, 24, 28, 41
Medicine, 135-36, 148-9
Medina, 52
Mediterranean, 21, 36, 41, 44
Meidan-i-Shah, 69
Meshed, 65, 69, 74, 79, 119, 124, 147
Mesopotamia, 11, 19
Mitanni, 19
Mithridates, 40; Mithridates V, 41
Mohammed, 51-54, 88-89, 114
Mohammed Reza, Shah Pahlavi (see Reza Shah)
Muharram, 89

Mongols, 61, 62, 64, 67
Moslems (see Islam)
Mosques, 59, 64, 70-71, 124
Mossadegh, Dr., 131
Mostahab, 52
Mountains, 12-17, 37, 96, 101-2, 110
Muhammad, 77, 78
Muhammad Ali Shah, 79
Museums: Archaeological, 30; Chehel Sotun, 71; crown jewels, 76
Music, 45-46, 86
Muzaffar ad-din Shah, 78, 79

Nadir Shah, 76
Naft-i-Safid, 130
Naft-i-Shah, 130, 132
Naqsh-i-Rustum, 43
Nasir-ad-din, 63-64
Nasr-ad-din, Shah, 78
National Iranian Company, 132
Navy, Iranian, 77, 82
Near East Foundation, 152
Nebuchadnezzar, 69
New Year (No-Ruz), 91-94, 114
Nizam al-Mulk, 58
Nizami, 59
Nordics, 18

Observatories, 57, 62, 64
Oil and gas, 29, 117, 129-132, 141
Olympius, 36
Omar, 54
Omar Khayyam, 57, 59

Pahlavi (dynasty), 80; (see also Language)
Pakistan, 136
Palaces, 44, 71, 97; Ataxerxes, 25; Chehel Sotun, 71; Ecbatana, 20; Firuzabad, 46; Ghazan Khan, 62; Gulistan, 91, 122; Marble, 122; Sargon, 20; Xerxes, 25
Parliament (see Majlis)

Parsa, 41
Parsus, 30-33, 55
Pasargadae, 26
Peacock Throne, 76
Persepolis, 22-26, 35, 38, 43, 44, 91, 125
Persian Gulf, 82, 95, 110, 130
Philip of Macedonia, 35, 36
Philosophers, 56, 59-59
Physicians, 62
PLAN, 132, 136-151
Poets, 56, 59, 62-3, 66, 67, 75
Point Four Program, 152
Population, 12, 16, 31, 105, 119, 141, 149

Qanat, 48-50
Qasr-i-Shirin, 47
Qavam ad-din, 64
Quasvin, 79

Railways, 78, 80, 82
Ramazan, 53, 89
Rashid ad-din, 62
Razi Serological Institute, 135, 136
Red Cross (Red Lion and Sun), 152
Reform program, 141-152
Religion and religious customs, 27, 33, 34, 41, 43, 46, 55, 57, 68, 74, 89; (see also Christians, Islam, Shi'a, Zoroastrianism)
Revolts, 40-41, 42-43, 58, 75, 79, 80, 102
Rey, 57, 60
Reza Shah, 65, 79-82, 102, 119, 139-151
Rezaieh, Lake, 14
Rig Veda, 28
Rivers, 14-15, 47; Danube, 21; Euphrates, 21; Kraun, 99; Oxus, 54; Tigris, 39; Zayandeh Rud, 14
Roads, 12, 14, 18, 21, 152
Rock carvings, 20, 43

Rome, 41, 43
Rosekhana, 89
Roshanak, 37
Rowzeh Khan, 89
Rudaki, 56
Rumi, 63
Russia, 12, 14, 64, 77-8, 79, 82, 103, 131

Sabzeh, 91-94
Sacred writings, 28, 31, 41, 56
Sa'di, 56, 62-3, 125
Safavid, 68
Saffarids, 56
Salaam, 122
Salamis, 21
Samanids, 56
Samarkand, 64
Sang-i-farsh, 18
Sanitation, 108, 115-116, 147-148
Sarbandan, 113
Sardis, 22
Sardsir, 101
Sargon, campaign, 20
Saruj, 115
Sarvistan, 46
Sassanians, 42, 44, 45, 46, 48, 50, 54, 55, 56, 91
Scientists, 56, 57, 59
Scythians, 23
Seleucia, 39
Seleucids, the, 38, 39, 40, 41
Seljuqs, 57, 58, 59
Sepehen, 69
Shahnama, 35, 45, 56, 60, 63, 69, 114
Shapur (city), 47
Shapur I, 43, 44, 46; Shapur II, 45
Shi'a, 55, 57, 68, 69
Shimron, 123
Shiraz, 22, 47, 62, 64, 65, 66, 76, 119, 125, 146
Shirley, Sir Anthony; Shirley, Robert, 75

J

Shushtar, 97, 98
Sistan, 64
Sizdah-Bedar, 93
"The Spring of Khosrau," 44
Sraosha, 30
Sudrah, 31
Suez Canal, 12
Susa, Susiana, 21, 22, 24, 41
Syria and Syrians, 23, 39, 136

Tabriz, 62, 68, 119, 146
Taharids, 56
Tahmureth, 69
Taj Mahal, 64
Tamerlane, 64
Tappe Yahya, 19
Taxes, 34
Tazzieh, 89
Teheran, 15, 16, 30, 57, 78, 79, 80, 85, 102, 119, 120, 122, 124, 127, 131, 135, 141
Tents, 95-97
Tombs, 60; Ali, 74, Cyrus, Daniel, 26, Ghazan Khan, 62, Imam Reza, 65, 124, Sa'di, 62, 125; Hafiz, 66-67, 125, Najaf, 74, Tughril Beg, 60
Tower of Silence, 32, 54
Trade routes, 12
Transportation, 93, 112, 120, 133
Tribes, 19, 40, 105; Arab, 103; Bakhtiari, 96, 98, 99, 102, 103; Cossacks, 78, 102; Goreish, 54; Khamseh Arabs, 96; Kuhgelu,

96; Kurds, 73, 96, 103; Lurs, 96, 102, 103; Parthians, 40-42, 56; Qajar, 77; Shah Savans, 72-3; Zand, 76
Tughril Beg, 57, 60
Turkey and Turks, 57, 68, 69, 136

UNICEF, 152
Universities, 128, 145, 146-147
Uzbecks, 69, 73

Valerian, 43
Venice, 62
Villages, 12, 14, 105-106, 109-110; Ancient, 18
Vogue, 127
Vohu Manah, 30

Water, 14, 16, 47-50; see also Irrigation
Weapons, 18, 24
White Revolution, 144
Women, 33, 81, 96, 98-99, 142-144
World War II, 82, 131, 134

Xerxes, 21, 22, 25, 30, 33

Yazishna, 31
Yezd, 16

Zoroaster, Zoroastrianism, 41, 52, 54, 55, 129; see also Parsus